# The Alpha Thief

## In Love with the Police Chief's Daughter

The Beginning

Volume 1

**Isaac King**

# TABLE OF CONTENT

# About Author

**About the Author: Isaac King**

Isaac King is a passionate storyteller with a talent for weaving romance, suspense, and raw emotion into compelling narratives. With a unique ability to create complex characters and unforgettable plots, Isaac's stories captivate readers and leave them yearning for more.

As the author of *The Alpha Thief: In Love with the Police Chief's Daughter*, Isaac embarks on an ambitious five-volume journey, exploring themes of love, loyalty, betrayal, and redemption. His writing is inspired by real-life struggles, deep human connections, and the enduring power of love to triumph over adversity.

Isaac King believes in the power of storytelling to transport readers to new worlds, challenge perspectives, and ignite imaginations. When he's not writing, Isaac enjoys connecting with his readers, finding inspiration in everyday life, and exploring the beauty of human relationships.

Stay connected with Isaac King for updates on his work, behind-the-scenes insights, and sneak peeks at upcoming volumes.

# Author's Note to Readers

Dear Readers,

Thank you for picking up *The Alpha Thief: In Love with the Police Chief's Daughter*. This story marks the beginning of an epic five-volume journey that delves into forbidden love, dangerous secrets, and the relentless pursuit of redemption.

In this first volume, you'll be introduced to Ryder, an Alpha living on the edge, caught between his life as a thief and his undeniable connection to the one person he should stay far away from—the Police Chief's daughter. Their story is one of passion and defiance, of two hearts colliding in a world determined to keep them apart.

As you turn the pages, expect twists that will keep you guessing, emotions that will tug at your heart, and characters whose choices will challenge everything you thought you knew about love and loyalty.

I'm thrilled to share this journey with you. Your support, reviews, and feedback inspire me to keep telling stories that capture the complexity of life and love.

Enjoy every moment, and get ready for the twists and turns ahead!

Sincerely,
**Isaac King**

# CHAPTER 1
## The Thief in the Night

To me, the night always seemed alive; every shadow served as a hiding spot, and every pulse warned.

I was the thief, whose name had become a whispered tale at both the police station and the underground.

I was not just any burglar. I didn't care much about the publicity. Every theft—every deliberate action—served the interests of my pack. Families.

Tonight, was much like other evenings.

Slung on the brink of a high-rise building, the city opened out like a map of possibilities. I bent. The benevolent elite was mixing in their sparkling gowns and fitted suits, and the gala was in full flow underneath, unaware of the predator hovering overhead.

I replaced the black leather gloves on my hands, my enhanced senses picking up bits of laughter and clinking glasses in the evening air.

Tonight, the daughter of the police chief was here.

Elena

I shouldn't have cared. She presented a complication I could not afford. Still, I knew I would spot her anywhere. Even from a distance, she was unusual, sharp, demanding, and a bit too driven for her own good. That type of fire was seductive, even though I knew it would burn me.

"Focus," I said under my breath, rejecting the idea as I looked down at the floor. My intended goal was not her. Tonight, it was something considerably more physical—a key card kept in the rear office of the gala site. Without it, Cain, my competitor, would have an advantage that I cannot tolerate.

Like a vulture seeking any vulnerability, Cain had been circling my pack. He would have destroyed everything I had created with one slip-up and one error.

I cannot let it pass by.

The falling was flawless. Sliding in via an unlocked maintenance window, I ascended the side of the building. Thick walls and heavy doors muted the noise of the event, and the world became silent. With delicate feet and steady breathing, I walked like a ghost.

However, even a ghost could not be perfect.

The sound of approaching heels stopped me mid-step. My pulse quickened, and as I slipped into the darkness, my muscles tightened.

She turned up.

Elena

 She had a profound impact on me. Her emerald-green dress draped her body in a way that made her appear both untouchable and dangerously close, her dark hair exquisitely twisted. Her keen eyes swept the hall, and for a second I feared she may have seen me.

She lacked, nevertheless.

She continued to stroll with assured motions and a high head. I almost laughed bitterly as my chest tightened. She had not been invited here. I wasn't meant to see her.

The scheme did not include this.

I waited until her heels stopped, then crept inside the office. Tucked within a sleek metal drawer, the key card was precisely where my information had said it would be. Simple.

Otherwise, it ought to have been.

I felt it—a change in the air, a warning prickling down my spine—the instant I touched it.

"freezes!"

As I turned, my keen sense of escape routes fully calculated, I came across Elena Hart, her green eyes now ablaze with rage. As I turned, my keen sense of escape routes fully calculated, I came across Elena Hart, her green eyes now ablaze with rage. Her posture remained constant as she clutched a stun gun in one hand.

Who the fuck are you? Her voice was low but forceful; she insisted.

I may have started to lie. I could have enchanted my path out. Rather, I grinned, a cocky edge creeping into my voice. Just a crook passing by.

Her stare sharpened, and for a moment I believed she may really shoot. She moved closer instead, her voice bursting with power. "What do you think you have just stepped into?"

For a brief moment, our conflict overshadowed everything else, including Cain, the pack, and the work. Even though I knew it would ruin me, all I could see was her, poised like a storm I wanted to swim into.

I softened my voice and added, "I could ask you the same thing." "Sweetheart, you're over your head."

Her jaw clenched at the term, and I nearly grinned. practically.

Before she could respond, the sound of approaching feet broke the moment. Strengthening elements Not tonight, not ever—you're not even able to afford to be caught.

My movements was swifter than she had expected. One hand sprang out, knocking the stun pistol from her hold, and the other softly but forcefully shoved her into the wall.

I apologized, my voice barely audible.

Then, I vanished like smoke into the evening.

Adrenaline continued to flow through me as I made my way back to the rooftop, peering down with the key card in hand. Achievements. However, my thoughts was not directed toward the task at hand. On her was they on.


Elena

I had not just taken a key card tonight. I had snatched a moment with her and wasn't sure I would ever get it back.

Benevolently, oblivious to the chaos I had left behind, the gala continued below. However, I couldn't shake the feeling that tonight had set something uncontrollably in motion.

Something hazardous.

# Chapter 2
## An Alpha View

I had fled, but the night stayed with me like a second skin, the meeting with Elena not going away from my thoughts. Every stride back to the den drew me towards the truth I couldn't escape—responsibility, threats, and a rival alpha breathing down my neck.

Still all I could see was her. She defied in her green eyes. Her heat when I had pressed her against that frigid wall.

I shook my head and pushed my thoughts back towards the key card in my pocket. It was leverage, a lifeline for my bag, not just some plastic.

Cain would prevail without it, and I could not enable that to happen. My pack included everything I had. All I could afford to give concern to.

As I moved, the roofs melted into a black mosaic. The city was alive with its usual anarchy: sirens in the distance, muted arguments pouring out of open windows, the buzz of a town never truly slept in. This city, this part of me, and yet I was invisible within it.

Tension permeated the air in the den when I arrived. My pack was family, linked by survival and desperation, not simply a collection of waswolves. However, today their eyes revealed they yearned for more than just survival. They needed hope.

"You understood it? My second-in-command, Milo, moved forward with a mixed-relief and tired look. Lean yet muscular, his wolf was always ready to battle just under the surface.

From my pocket, I withdrew the key card and threw it across the room's middle table." Got it.

Though it was clear that my group exhaled collectively, the uncertainties that lingered in their eyes was not eliminated. They trusted me, but trust was limited when survival was on the line.

"This buys us time," I responded, my voice calm, demanding. "Cain will not move without this."

"Time for what, Ryker?" Milo spoke in a strong, annoyed tone. He's not going to quit. You're aware of? And we cannot stay in hiding indefinitely.

I fired back, my alpha presence exploding, not cowering. Milo flinched, but I lowed my voice before going on. We'll work things out. As always.

Milo nodded, but our mutual tension persisted. He had nothing to be incorrect. Cain's threat was a noose tightening around every one of our necks. I could not, however, exhibit frailty. Not now.

"Ryker..."" A calmer voice emerged from the conflict, and I turned to see the youngest pack member, Lily. Her wide eyes revealed concern. "What if he discovers us?"""

"He won't." My response was instinctive, but the reality was heavier than I could have let on. There would not be a struggle if Cain discovered us. There would be murder.

Later that evening, I was standing on the brink of the rooftop with a city view. Sharp, the wind carried the smell of rain and far-off danger. Restless, my wolf awoke inside of me.

Her face came back in my memory. Elena." Her voice, harsh and uncompromising, wanting to know who I was, still audible to me.

I hadn't expected her to see through the gaps in my mask, nor to run across her. What she made me feel was dangerous. Dangerous and unachievable.

I turned around, not sure it was Milo because I heard a faint sound behind me. He moved deliberately and with weight. He always showed respect by making sure I knew he was arriving.

You're distracted, he remarked straightforwardly.

"I'm good."

Sure you're. He stood up next to me, looking out over the city. "You're thinking about her..."

I didn't reply. Milo understood me too well; denial of it would just make things worse.

"She's having problems, Ryker."

Knowing.

"She's also the daughter of the police head.

"I am aware of it as well."

Milo groaned and ran a hand over his hair. You're running with fire here. Cain's breath down our necks, and you're... what? Considering a female who, should she know the truth, would turn you in?

"She doesn't know the truth," I said, my voice sharper than I wanted. And she's not simply a girl.

Milo raised his eyebrows, but he refrained from pushing farther. Rather, he looked at me with equal parts annoyance and sympathy. Just keep sight of what counts.

He went without saying another word, and I appreciated the quiet that followed. But his comments stayed, biting at the margins of my consciousness.

The next day I cannot avoid her.

The cosmos, or destiny, or whatever merciless power controlled my existence, appeared ready to toss us together.

Instead of staking out Cain's next action, I found myself on high alert at the brink of a packed marketplace.

Before I saw her, the familiar aroma of her perfume assaulted me; when I turned, she was there.

She was standing beside a vendor, her black hair free around her shoulders, her face austere as she asked someone. She was working, I understood, gathering data like a predator hunting.

I ought to have started to go. Should have kept in the background. But I failed to.

I blurted before I could stop myself, "Elena."

She turned, her eyes tightening at the sight of me. She seemed surprised for a single second, then something sharper soon took front stage. Question.

"You," she murmured, her voice low and laced with steel. "This's where you're working?

"Shopping," I murmured, throwing her a smile I could feel.

Her lips drew a thin line, then she moved in front. You're lying.

I bent my head to let her see the brink of my pleasure. "You don't believe me? I feel wounded.

"I hardly know you at all."

Her proximity now, too close, caused my wolf to rise once more in response, clenching my fists.

The words was out before I could stop them, and for a while we simply gazed at one another, the surroundings blurring into nothing. Maybe you should.

Her mouth closed, and she shook her head. Back off. Her voice colder now, she added, "Stay out of my way."

I felt her words weigh down on me as she turned and left. Still, one thing was clear even as I watched her go.

I was not planning to linger in her path.

And something informed me she was not staying out of me.

# Chapter 3
# Elena's Will

 Some women inherit jewels or family recipes. I took over a tireless search for justice.

Although my father always believed I had too much heart for this area of work, he was unaware it sharpened me. More propelled.

Not here to be the ideal daughter or the next rookie detective living in his shadow. I came here to establish myself.

Which was why the events of last night—him—we're chewing at me.

The gala was meant to be basic. Beautiful gowns, dull presentations, and an opportunity to socialize with the political elite of the city. Rather, I came across a burglar who moved like fog and had eyes that made me doubt what I knew about crooks.

Ryder

Though I didn't know his name yet, that smug smile stayed with me. He had passed through my fingers, leaving just a bolt of annoyance and an unquenchable burning.

Now seated in my father's office, I handed over the gala security video. Although it had taken some coaxing to acquire access to these files, I was not allowing him to ignore this.

Elena, what search are you looking for? From behind his desk, my father questioned with a dubious voice.

"A lead," I said, looking over the blurry video. He was audacious enough to turn up for the gala. He must be confident, as this implies perhaps too sure.

Arranging his arms over his chair, my father reclined back. His emblem sparkled in the sunshine coming through the window. To me, he had always been bigger than life—stoic, austere, the type of guy who made you stand a bit straighter merely entering the room. Still, recently cracks was beginning to appear.

With a stern voice, he urged, "Let it go." "We have more issues to handle than some thieves."

Unable to keep the fury out of my voice, I shot back, "This thief is making a fool of us." "You're advising me to ignore him; he's been sliding between the gaps for months.""

"I'm telling you to give priorities top importance," he said, his voice like steel. "Real criminals are out there, Elena. Risky ones.

And why do you find this man to not be dangerous?"'

He ignored her, and that quite conveyed more than words could ever have.

Following leads, I spent the remainder of the day, but by nightfall I was no closer to locating him. Every path came to a dead end, every testimony erratic and untrustworthy. It was aggravating.

And suddenly he was here. His movements, the way his words stayed in my thoughts like an echo I couldn't shake.

Though I wanted to keep it hidden, there was something about him. Something else caused my pulse to speed, not just out of wrath but also something else.

I dismissed the idea and went to the Lower District, the one location I knew would provide solutions.

The streets here was not at all like the polished districts I had grown up in. They was alive in various ways, vibrating with the type of energy that, if improperly navigated, might be fatal.

Though I felt eyes on me, I maintained my head up and confident walk. This was not my first visit here; early on I had discovered that hesitancy was a weakness you could not afford.

My aim was a tavern hidden in a dark nook of the city, the type of place where secrets was money and the incorrect enquiry could kill you.

Inside, the quiet hum of voices mixed with dense smoke. I looked across the room and focused on a guy seated at the bar—a known source who tended to have loose lips when appropriately motivated.

I slipped down to the seat next to Danny.

He raised his bloodshot eyes harrowingly and realized something. "Hart," you know, my reputation suffers somewhat when you show your presence here.

"Neither is hiding information," I said, keeping my voice laid back. "I'm seeking someone.

Danny laughed and leant back to sip his drink slowly. Not all of us, however."'

I moved a picture across the bar, a single frame from the gala video. Tell me who he's, please.

Danny's attitude altered. subtle but clearly identifiable. She identified him.

"Can't help you," he answered, shoving back the picture.

I leant in, Danny said, lowering my voice to a menacing whisper. "Games do not appeal to me right now. Tell me all you know; then, I will make sure every police officer in this city finds you precisely where you're.

His jaw clenched, and for a few seconds I thought he may flee. He groaned again, running a palm over his face.

"Fine," he said in a whisper. But you missed hearing it from me.

An hour later I was standing on the outskirts of the city besides a deserted warehouse. Danny said here I would discover my thief—or at least someone who knew him.

The air smelled of rain, the sky gloomy and weighty. I dropped inside, my beam slicing through the darkness. The area was absolutely silent, the type of silence that made the hair on the rear of your neck rise up.

I walked deliberately, my senses sharp. Every floorboard squeak and shadow movement seemed like a menace.

I later heard it as well.

Deep and guttural, a rumbling growl emanating from someplace ahead. As I grabbed the flashlight, my heart raced in my chest.

"Who's there? I answered, my voice calm even though I was running on excitement.

None.

I moved forward; the roar became louder. Then he materialized, emerging from the darkness like a predator seeking its target.

His name was it.


Ryder

But something else now, something I hadn't seen at the gala. His eyes shone slightly in the darkness, an odd, wolfish color. His presence was more dominant.

Neither of us moved momentarily. Unspoken tension filled the air between us.

"This's where you're working? His voice was low and menacing as he inquired.

I fired back, attempting to hide the way my pulse surged and ask the same question.

He grinned, the same confident, nasty smile from the gala. I will say you have guts. But love, you're engaged in a deadly game.

I snapped, coming forward and saying, "Don't call me that."

His smile vanished, and for a minute something almost vulnerable flashed in his face.

"You ought to go," he replied gently. "Your world is not this one."

I said, "I'm making this my world."

The words lingered in the air, and for a brief while I thought he may say anything else. But suddenly the moment was broken by the sound of feet echoing throughout the warehouse.

Ryker's face became stiff, and he grabbed my arm to drag me into the darkness just as a group of guys walked into the room.

His breath warm on my ear, he said, "They're not here for you." Still, they won't give a damn if they come across you.

I had no time to dispute. Armed and with quiet, strained voices, the guys proceeded across the warehouse.

Ryker guided me through the labyrinth of goods and equipment, his motions swift and stealthy. His hold on my arm tightened.

The crisp night air slapped me like a slap as we at last slid out a side door. I drew my arm free and turned to face him.

"What the heck was that? I begged.

Your first and last warning," he added, his voice cooler now. "Stay clear of this, Elena. You're beyond your comprehension.

Then he vanished into the evening like a phantom.

But I left him behind. Not quite sure.

# Chapter 4

## Slights in the Shadow

The city spoke secrets. Whispers permeated its alleyways, rooftops, and subterranean dens, each darkness hiding a reality none wanted exposed.

Tonight, I was the darkness itself, not just one of those secrets.

Her kept me from stopping to ponder about.

Hart, Elena. Her name kept coming back to me as I negotiated the maze of streets; her resistance stayed like an unresolved challenge.

She had followed me into a world not fitting for her, but something told me she would keep returning. It was perilous. For her. For me. For everybody.

Her existence unknown to the pack. They wouldn't know. She would be seen by them as a danger, a diversion, or worse—an opportunity for Cain.

But I was smarter. She was not a danger. She burned too brilliantly to be overlooked. She was fire.

The idea made my chest constrict, so I had to force myself to concentrate. Tonight, I had a purpose that would not offer diversion.

I encountered Milo outside the entrance of a closed metro tunnel. His face was austere, his keen eyes looking around before he spoke.

"Your late arrival."

I passed him saying, "I'm here."

Before us the dark and wet tunnel opened out. Though the air smelled strongly of mildew and rust, under it was something more. something primordial.

Milo dropped into stride alongside me, his voice quiet. Cain has begun moving his pieces. He has a major project under way.

"He's always planning something," I said.

This's not the same. He's hiring outside of the city. Notes. Separations. He's assembling an army.

I paused and turned to face him. "Why nowadays?"

Milo paused, and I noticed the flutter of discomfort in his eyes. "He finds you to be weak, Ryker. That you seem preoccupied.

 My wolf rumbling under the surface, I closed my fists. "I'm not weak..."

Then prove it; Milo's voice was harsh and demanding. "You have recently missed work. The pack sees it. I perceive it. Whatever is dragging your attention, you must let it go.

I omitted responding. Not could.

Given his rightness.

Deeper down the caverns, the data guided us to a concealed stash Cain had been employing for weapon storage.

Eliminating it would be a little victory, a reminder that I wasn't only watching while he tightened his hold.

As we neared, the air got cooler and the faint buzz of voices came to me. Senses sharpening, I signaling Milo to halt.

"There are four of them," I said quietly. 'Armed.' Two inside, two by the door.

Milo nodded with a stern look. "What do you have in mind?

"Make division and conquer."

We moved softly and rapidly. The first two guards missed us approaching. One crumpled beneath Milo's fists; I took one down with a fast punch to the neck.

Two from within was more than ready. One of them drew a pistol, but I disarmed him before he could shoot.

I was quicker. Milo was ready; the other sprang at him, their combat a whirl of fists and snarls.

It passed in a few short seconds.

My breath consistent, I stood over the unconscious corpses. The surge of adrenaline coursed through me and was known. It grounded.

But a fresh idea entered my head when I examined the weapon stash.

Cain was equipping not just himself. He was getting ready for conflict.

The pack was wild by the time I got back to the lair. Although the raid had raised spirits, it had not eliminated the underlying anxiety as word of it had travelled.

Lily came up to me as I entered; her huge eyes begged for enquiries.

"Did you search and discover anything?

"Nothing we lacked knowledge of," I said.

She nodded, but her countenance clearly showed uncertainty. The pack was losing trust, and I had no idea how much longer I could keep them together.

I was alone myself in the little room I designated when the others retired for the evening. A reminder of the bigger game I was playing, the key card from the gala rested on the table.

Finally, there was her.

Elena in that warehouse, her fire, her will, stayed with me. She had gone too near, more than anybody else had ever done.

It was more than just risky. It was foolish.

Still, I knew I wouldn't be able to persuade myself to stay away.

Elena

Sitting outside the station in my vehicle, the night opened out before me like an unresolved riddle. Though it had left me shook, the warehouse encounter had also set something in motion in me.

He was not just a burglar. His eyes revealed it, as did his movement. He had something basic, something that defied the tidy, organized society I had grown up in.

And I could not let it go.

Not understanding was my father's attitude. The warehouse raid was rejected by him as just another dead end, another waste of money.

Nonetheless, I knew better. Ryker is more than simply a burglar. He was the secret to something more, something I still have to work out.

Pulling out my phone, I went over the pictures I had shot of the warehouse. Something I had overlooked had to be a hint.

I later saw that as well.

a symbol carved on the wall close to the spot I had challenged him. Though it was weak, nearly imperceptible, it was there—a crescent moon twisted with the head of a wolf.

As I gazed at it, my heart surged as the pieces of a jigsaw I knew nothing about started to fit.

Ryker was concealing something more than just pilfers of big stakes or stolen commodities.

It was something more profoundly ingrained.

Something harmful.


Ryner

Though the pack was sleeping, I couldn't relax. My head was a tempest, every idea louder than the next. Cain. The weaponry. the pack.

Her:

I moved outdoors, the chilly night air cutting over my flesh. Before me the city opened out like a sea of shadows and lights. It was suffocating even if its anarchy was wonderful.

My wolf moved restlessly, and I felt the familiar pull of the transformation. Still, I objected. not here. Not at this moment.

Rather, I allowed my senses to extend to listen to the city's pulse.

I sensed it then as well.

Her.

Elena was quite near. Too closely.

I tensed, my instincts ablaze. She came behind me.

Nice.

Allow her.

She would have to go further into the darkness if she was seeking my secrets.

She would also discover the truth there just waiting for her.

# Chapter 5
# A Meeting by Chance

Ryner

My regular haunt was not the café. very crowded and too exposed. Tonight, however, I had to fit in and seem as normal as could be.

Sensing great alertness, I moved into a booth in the rear. Fresh coffee mixed with customer conversation covered the stress coiling in my stomach.

My appointment with the guy was late. He was supposed to deliver me intelligence on Cain's next action, but in my world, lateness usually indicated betrayal—or worse.

My fingertips softly tapping the table, I watched the door. Every instinct urged me to go, yet something pulled me back—a need I was unable to overlook.

She then started to stroll in.

Elena:

The air changed the instant she arrived, as if the city itself was holding its breath. She was not dressed in her regular formal wear; today she wore black jeans and a leather jacket and let her hair free about her shoulders. She seemed... perilous.

And way too fascinating as well.

I descended farther into my booth, slanted slightly to evade her line of sight. She was not here, not now; this was not the moment to show up.

But time was not important to destiny.

She ordered coffee and looked around, her eyes keen and probing. She was not here for the atmosphere, very obviously.

She was a hunter.

And the hair on the back of my neck pricked as her gaze fixed on me.

Elena

Not meant to be here was I. Though I reminded myself twelve times on the way over, I couldn't avoid it.

I had come here, to this unassuming café on the brink of the Lower District, from the symbol I had discovered in the warehouse.

Though it seemed a long shot, something said I might discover solutions tonight.

Alternatively, someone.

I later saw him.

He was attempting to conceal, but he was not someone you could mistake. Riker. The pilfers. The mystery that has been stalking my ideas since the gala.

My pulse thumping in a manner I chose not to admit, I grabbed my coffee and headed towards his seat.

Sliding onto the seat opposite from him before he could react, I replied, "Fancy seeing you here."

His eyes locked with mine, and for a brief instant the globe collapsed to just the two of us. He had a magnetic quality that made it difficult to turn away.

"Elena," he whispered, his voice silky and quiet. "To what do I owe the pleasure?

"I could ask you the same question," I fired back. "What would a crook like you be doing in a location like this? The"

His grace infuriated me. "Coffee's excellent.

Leaning in slightly, I replied, "You're lying." You have someone waiting for you. That's who?

His face changed, a flutter of something I could not quite identify. For someone who ought to be arresting me, you're rather interested.

"Maybe I'm just here for the coffee," I responded, mirroring his smile with one of mine.

He chuckled, a subdued sound that made my back shudder. Are you not going to let this go?

"Not a chance.

Rye

She was hazardous in a manner I never would have predicted. Not just because she was brilliant and tenacious but also because she made me want to tell her everything.

And it presented difficulties as well.

"Elena," I murmured, my voice soft now. "You ought to stop." You're pursuing something you cannot grasp.

Then make me understand, she said, staring straight at me.

I failed. Not without escalating her risk over her current level.

The café door opened before I could answer, and I sensed the change right away. Two males came in, their motions too slow and their eyes too fixed.


Men by Cain

Bad it.

"Elena," I continued, sounding now rather urgent. You have to go. now.

'What? She scowled and looked over at the visitors.

I growled, already standing to go.

But it was already too late.


Elena

I could feel the tension in the air; Ryker's warning was not necessary to realize something was up. The two guys who had just arrived walked deliberately; their eyes swept the space until they settled on his.

And finally, on me.

Friends of yours? Keeping a calm voice, I asked.

Not exactly, he said, his mouth tense.

The males came forward with predatory attitudes. Ryker's hand shot out, halting me as I grabbed for my phone.

"Don't," he insisted. "They're observing..."

And what action do you propose we take?"

His smile came back, but it was slanted towards something darker this time. "We improvised."

He rose, bringing me to my feet before I could object. Too late, I understood what he was doing as his arm slid around my waist.

"Play along," he said, his lips touching my ear.

Stopped a few feet away, the two guys wore icy, calculated looks.

One of them, Ryker, whispered in a hushed voice. "Boss is looking for a term.

Ryker's nonchalant but deadly tone increased his hold on me. Tell Cain I'm busy, she said.

The man's eyes turned to mine, and I could see the identification in them. "This hers?" The"

She?

Before Ryker reacted, his free hand grabbed the guy by the collar and slammed him into the closest wall, so I had no time to consider what it meant.

Does one have to repeat oneself? He snipped, his deep rumble sending a shiver down my spine.

The second guy grabbed something—probably a weapon—but I was quicker, kicking his leg out from beneath him and sending him tumbling to the ground.

Ryker looked at me, a flutter of astonishment visible in his eyes. Not horrible.

Thank you; I was out of breath.

We left not to linger to see what came next. Ryker reached for my hand, yanking me out the rear door into the alley.

Rye

She was going to die right now.

Her hand in mine, as we ran across the alley, that was my first thought. She had no idea what she was handling—what Cain was capable of.

But hell, if she fell behind.

When we halted at last, I staggered against the brick wall trying to regain my breath. Elena stood next to me, her eyes ablaze with a mixture of defiance and exhilaration.

"Care to clarify what exactly happened? She asked.

"No," I said sharply.

Ryker—"

"Elena, stop," I said, my voice sterner than I had meant.

 "You're in over your head."

And whoever is responsible for that? She pulled back.

I responded with nothing. I cannot.

Given her accuracy.

Elena

He was irritating.

He was frightened, but as well. I could see it in the way his jaw tightened and his eyes flicked towards the darkness as if he was anticipating an assault right now.

Ryker participated in more than I could have imagined.

I also refused to let him deal with it by himself.

Fine, I responded, crossing my arms. "I will figure it out myself if you will not tell me."

"Don't," he hissed, his voice low and lethal.

"Why not?" asked Because it's much too dangerous? Since I am just the helpless little cop's daughter?

His eyes fixed on mine, and I felt as if he may blow up momentarily. Then his face relaxed just a little.

"Because you'll wind up in Cain's crosshairs if you keep digging," he warned softly. And he will not hesitate to murder you.

There was a heavy stillness between us, full of topics neither of which we were ready to discuss.

Then he turned, like a shadow, vanishing into the evening.

But I left him behind.

Not yet.


# Chapter 6
## Plan of the Police Chief

Elena

I was not trusted by my father. He never stated it straightforwardly, but I could sense it in his eyes and heard it in the clipped tone he used every time I mentioned Ryker's.

 Too emotionally engaged to think rationally, he believed I was chasing shadows.

About the emotional aspect, he was correct.

Ryker had gotten under my skin in ways I wanted not to acknowledge. That did not imply, however, that I was blind.

When Cain's guys arrived at the café, I sensed the tension in the air and had seen the emblem in the warehouse.

Ryker was in the core of something large that was happening.

"Elena, are you listening?"

Blinking, I concentrated on my father. Old coffee and leather heavily permeated his office as we was there. Arm crossed, he reclined back in his chair, his badge shining beneath the overhead lamp.

I said, "I'm listening," in a tone more pointed than I had meant.

His brow sank. Tell me what you believe then.

Meeting his eye, I responded, "I think you're underestimating this." Ryker is not just a small-time crook. He's in touch with something more, something deadly.

"Dangerous for him," my father shot back. "He's playing a game he doesn't understand, and when it catches up to him, it won't end well."

For us, too, I replied softly.

The jaw of my father contracted." What is it meant to imply?

Leaning back in my chair, I responded, "Nothing." "Forget it."

I could not forget it, however. Something hidden in the lines of strain on his face, he was not sharing with me. Although my father was a fortification, even fortifications was not perfect.

Ryker

I had run out of time.

Cain's preparations was becoming more ambitious, and my pack was getting restless. They averted my eyes, so I could sense their uncertainty even if they didn't express it straightforwardly. An alpha who neglected his own was not really an alpha at all.

Standing in the alley behind the den, I could smell rain and could just hear the city humming. A minute later Milo came to meet me, his face stern.

He exclaimed, cutting off the politeness: "We have to act."

Knowing.

And yet you're still unsure.

I looked at him, but he refused to back off.

"We cannot wait for Cain to move first," he said. Should we, do it? It's over.

He was correct, but acting now meant running everything on a gamble. Making a mistake would not be affordable. Not working with Cain. Not including Elena.

Surely not with anything her father had in mind either.


Elena.

Though I had little option, I disliked following after my father's rear. His adamant denial of the wider picture was going to cause deaths.

Digging through old case files, searching for anything that would link Ryker to the bigger network of crimes my father had been discreetly constructing a case against, I spent the rest of the day Every lead broke the minute I came near, like following smoke.

And then I came across it.

One report hidden amid a stack of unresolved cases with a known symbol scratched in the margin.

Head of the wolf with the crescent moon.

As I went over the report, my tummy turned over. It went beyond Ryker as well. It has to do with his pack.

And my father knew as well.


Ryker

The knock on the den door was too deliberate and too harsh. My muscles tightened for a battle as I opened it and ordered the others to keep back. Nevertheless, it wasn't Cain. Elena spoke first.

"This's where you're working? I snarled and dragged her inside before anybody saw her.

Her voice low but firm, she replied, "We need to talk."

I had no time for this. Not a good moment right now.

"Set aside time."

Her eyes blazed with a will that made my chest contract. Whatever this was, it transcended my own experience.

I guided her into a more sedate section of the lair, apart from the others.

Talk, I replied.

She stopped, looking around the room, then back at me. "Your pack. There are known to my father.

The words strike me like a gut-reversing blow.

"What?"

She added, "He's been building a case against you." Not just yourself. Every one of you.

My wolf roused, a roar vibrating within me. This was terrible. Worse than what I had imagined.

"Why are you approaching me with this? My voice subdued, I asked.

Her eyes locked on mine. "Because I don't think you're the real enemy," she replied. You have to prove it, however.


Elaine

Ryker did not answer straight away. He just stood there, his jaw clenched and his eyes a tempest of feelings I was unable to interpret.

"You trust me not," I replied.

You're correct, he said. I don't.

Though the remarks wounded more than they ought to have, I persisted.

Then rely on yourself, I said. "It's over if you let my father make the initial approach."

His eyes softened, only a little. "Why do you find yourself doing this? "

Not wanting to watch him collapse. Because I couldn't get rid of the impression that he was hiding from us more than he revealed.

Because I gave it some thought.

None of it, however, I could say.

"Because it's the right thing to do," I said instead.

Ryder

Her comments lingered in the air, and for a time I wanted to believe her. To believe she was not come to use me, to trap me.

But I could not afford luxury like trust.

Still, her admonition was impossible to ignore. I had to find out quickly what her father was planning—what exactly?

You shouldn't be here, I said.

She opened her arms. Still here, however.

I nearly let out a grin. practically.

Milo showed up at the doorway with a grim look before I could reply.

We have an issue, he added.

Of course, we do, I said quietly.


Elena

Though I had no idea what I anticipated, it was not this.

Milo brought us to a room bursting with maps and security images. One picture drew me in: a hazy picture of my father exiting a conference with someone I cannot identify.

"Who is that? I questioned, pointing at the figure.

"Someone we have been observing," Milo remarked. "He labored for Cain."

My blood became frigid.

Ryker replied, his voice like a razor, "Your father's not just building a case." He's acting on both sides.

Like a goods train, the insight came over me. Not only was my father chasing Ryker. He was making use of him.

And so was I right now.

We put together what we could, but the night dragged on, and the responses only begged more questions. My head was a whirl of uncertainty and doubt by the time I left the den.

Ryker guided me to the alley's brink, his presence anchoring in a manner I didn't want to acknowledge.

"Be careful," he cautioned, his voice lower now.

You also, I answered.

Our eyes locked for a time, and I sensed something in his look that I couldn't quite identify.

And then he vanished into the darkness.

But the secrets we had unearthed was not keeping quiet.

Not for very long.

# Chapter 7
## Hazard in the Alley

Ryker

The night was cooler than normal, the frost stinging at my skin as I walked along the Lower District's little lanes.

The persistent tension in the air, like a warning prickle down my spine, remained unabated. This was not one more evening. I could sense that something was about to happen.

Tonight, wasn't about Milo, who had been advocating for action and revenge against Cain's escalating threat.

Tonight, was Survival Evening. I had to travel quickly, keeping ahead of the murmurs starting to surround my pack and myself.

Still, my thoughts turned to her even as I concentrated on the current work.


Elena

She was a hazard, a diversion, yet I could not resist the draw. It was enticing to witness her passion and the way she maintained her position despite knowing who I was. I couldn't, however, afford to lose concentration. Not now.

I halted at a bend, instincts flying. The alley ahead was eerily silent and motionless. Here, the shadows appeared to be deeper, and the air was thicker.

Then I heard it—the soft scraping of a boot across concrete.

"Show yourself," I replied, speaking softly and steadily.

One person emerged from the shadows with careful motions. He was big and tall; the hood of his jacket covered half of his face. To know him, however, I did not have to see his face.

"Cain," I screamed.

He smiled, a smile that made my inner wolf yearn for freedom. "Evening, Ryker. Strolling around right now?

"What is your desired outcome?"

"Isn't it clear? "He moved forward, his presence sweeping the passageway like a tempest. "I am looking for what is mine."

I twisted to strike, my hands tightly clenched. "You have nothing here."

"Not yet," he responded, his voice laid back and somewhat sarcastic. However, it appears that you're simplifying the situation. You're getting distracted, losing focus, and even your pack is starting to doubt you.


He successfully penetrated my mind. However, I won't allow him to see it.


"Stay out of my way," I said, projecting an air of authority.

"Or what?" asked? Cain's grin became broader. You're going to stop me? Ryker, let me say it straightforwardly.

You're beyond your field of expertise. Playing home with the police chief's daughter keeps you too occupied to notice what's ahead.

With rage blurring my eyes, I lunged before I could stop myself.

Elena

I had not intended to follow him. I told myself I was only on my way home, that the tug in my chest was not pointing me in his direction, but I could not lie to myself indefinitely.

Ryker

Something about him made me forget everything I knew, something that defied reason. This dangerous burglar was more than what people thought.

And I was hungry for the truth.

I stopped upon turning a bend. I noticed him ahead in the low light of the alley. But he was not by himself.

Another guy stood opposite him, taller, more expansive, his presence exuding threat. I could hear their words despite their physical tension.

Then Ryker moved, quicker than I could have imagined.

In a flurry of action, his body collided with another man.

I never considered it. I responded recently.


Ryker

Cain was stronger than I had recalled; his fists landed with sufficient power to cause me to trip. I was not, however, backing down. Not now.

"You're weak," he growled, slamming his knee into my ribs. Always have been.

I clenched my teeth, utilizing the agony to propel me forward. I grabbed his arm, whirling it behind his back, then slammed him into the wall.

I snapped, "You talk too much."

He chuckled, the sound deep and menacing. "And you're still holding back. Go forth, Ryker. Let the wolf run away.

I paused, and that was all he needed. He spun to meet me with a predatory smile.

He continued, his voice full of assurance, "You cannot win this." "Not like this."

A strange aroma assaulted me before I could reply: familiar and out of context.


Elena;

She arrived here.


Elena

I was unsure of my own thoughts. Probably the worst thing I had done was charge into the midst of a brawl between two obviously non-normally behaved males.

But something ignited within me as I watched Ryker stumble.

Stop! Stepping into the alley, I screamed.

Men stopped; their eyes locked on mine. While the other guy, Cain, peered over me with a disconcerting interest, Ryker's countenance was a combination of amazement and rage.

"Well, well, Cain said," his voice like silk. "What do we have right now?"

Ryker hissed and walked between us. "Leave her out of this."

Cain laughed, still staring at me. "She's nice, Ryker. I understand your potential for distraction.

Ryker growled. "Touch her, and I'll kill you," Ryker said in a low, deadly voice.


Cain clearly took pleasure in lifting his eyebrow. "Considerate, Ryker. You're starting to sound like a leader again.

Then he vanished into the darkness as quickly as he had first emerged.


Ryker

The quiet that followed was intolerable. With my heart thumping and my mind spinning, I turned to Elena.

What on earth are you doing here? I asked, my voice rougher than I wanted.

Her eyes flaming with wrath, she yelled out, "I could ask you the same thing."

Trying to quiet the turmoil within me, I ran a hand through my hair. "This isn't your world, Elena. You ought not to be here.

Still now, here I am.

Her protest infuriated me. And intoxicated.

What did you just step into? I asked, approaching closer."

Not backtracking, she answered, "I know enough." "That was Cain, was it not? That's the individual you've been attempting to thwart.

I didn't respond.

She continued, "Ryker," her voice weaker now. "You can believe me."

I should have desired. God, I want to. However, I cannot afford the luxury of trust.

I turned aside and replied, "Go home, Elena."

She replied, snatching my arm, "No."

I paused, and her touch shocked me.

Her voice calm, "I'm not going anywhere," she added. Not until you speak the truth.


Elena

In his eyes, I could see the war—that conflict between wanting to drive me away and wanting to guard me.

"Please," I pleaded, my voice barely audible. "I am here to help you."

I momentarily believed he may allow me inside. He shook his head, suddenly yanking his arm free.

His voice flat, he answered, "You cannot."

He vanished into the evening before I could reply, leaving me alone with myself in the alley.

But I wasn't finished.

Still to come.

# Chapter 8
## Stress in Pack Tensions

Ryker

When I got back the den was humming. Every word expressed in irritation, every glance sharpened by uncertainty, the air was tense.

Before I heard Milo's, voice filling the clamor and asking for control I couldn't provide, I hadn't even gone through the door.

"Silence! I smiled, my voice tinged with the alpha command. The room became quiet right away, and several hundred eyes fixed on me.

From Lily's frightened face to Milo's barely hidden wrath, I let my eyes fly over them. My group. My share of the work. But tonight their allegiance seemed brittle, like a thread just about to break.

"What is occurring? Keeping a cool head but a strong voice, I asked

Milo moved forward, his mouth tightly locked. " Cain has been returning to our land. Two of his guys was snooping close by the warehouses.

And so on."


"And we're tired of waiting, Ryker," Milo remarked, his voice firm but tinged with irritation. We must act before he separates us.

With the weight of their expectations firmly on my shoulders, I closed my fists. They want retaliation and action. But a careless action directed against Cain may cost us everything.

We will deal with Cain, I replied. But we do it on our terms, not his.

Murmurs of agreement and discontent mixed through the group. Milo continued without faltering, his eyes fixed on me.

"What prevents us? "He asked for. "Why do we usually react instead of countering? Are you waiting for him to wipe out our existence? The "

Low and warning, a growl tore across my chest. "Watch your tone, Milo."

He stared at me for a time then turned away, but the difficulty stayed in the air. Watching to see how I would approach this was the pack.

"We lose by playing his game," I remarked with a stern voice. "Cain wants us to act out of rage. He desires errors made by us. We're not less intelligent than that. more powerful than that.

Though I could see uncertainty flickering in their eyes, I also saw optimism.


Elena

Out of my brain, I could not get the expression in Ryker's eyes. Like he was ready to travel the whole globe to protect me, he had stepped between Cain and me.

It was irresponsible and upsetting, something I could not overlook.

But just now I had more major issues to cope with.

As I looked deeper into my father's argument against Ryker's pack, I came to see how deadly it was. He was creating a trap, not only collecting evidence.

Confirming that was the files I had taken from his office. He understood the group, their motions, their weaknesses. He intended to pull Cain out into the open using them as bait.

And Ryker ended up in the midst.

I couldn't permit that to transpire.


Ryker

Though the flock had scattered, the stress remained. Milo lingered behind, his arms crossed and he observed me with an expression that seemed almost rebellious.

His voice low, he replied, "You're holding back."

I shot back, "I'm keeping us alive."

"At what expenses?""

My wolf rising to the surface drove me on. "You believe I don't want to call this off? That I do not lay awake every night considering strategies to halt Cain? But we're destroyed if we make one mistake.

And then, should we do nothing? Milo responded differently.

For that I lacked a response.

Lily came inside the creaking door, her wild eyes darting between us. " Ryker," she murmured, her voice little. Someone is come to see you.

My chest contracted. "who?"—

She thought twice. "It's her.


Elena

Coming into the den, I had no idea what I anticipated. Perhaps suspicion and animosity. I was not prepared for the weight of so many eyes on me, the obvious tension in the room the instant I entered.

Ryker was at the heart of everything; his presence commanded even amid the tumult. When he spotted me, his countenance changed to combine annoyance with something I couldn't really describe.

"Elena," he added, speaking softly.

We need to chat, I murmured, avoiding the inquisitive looks from his pack.

His tone tight, he said, "This isn't a good time."


Holding his eye, I murmured, "Make time."

The pack murmured, and Ryker's jaw clenched. Give us a minute, he urged, his voice bearing weight of authority.

The group paused then filed off, leaving us by ourselves.

"This's where you're working? His irritation clear as he urged.

"Your pack is in danger," I remarked, approaching closely. "My dad is going to get to Cain using you. You're marching straight for the trap he's lying.

His eyes contracted. "How do you find out that?"

"Because I saw the files," I said. " Ryker, he's observing you. He knows more than you would believe.

He hardly answered for a second. Though his face was inscrutable, I could see the wheels churning in his head.

"Why are you approaching me with this? At last he inquired.

"Because I don't want to see you get hurt," I blurted, the words flowing out before I could stop them.

His look softened, just a little. Quietly, he murmured, "You shouldn't be here."

And yet here I am, I answered.

Ryker

She was unrelenting. Reluctant, careless, and too damned courageous for her own benefit. Still, I couldn't deny the truth in her remarks as much as I wanted to send her away.

I wanted to know what her father was planned if he was organizing anything.

Tell me everything, I said.

She paused, her eyes darting over mine. Only if you swear to pay attention.

I nodded and she started to speak.

Her completion caused my thoughts to fly. Should what she claimed be accurate, we was more under risk than I had thought.

My pack was trapped in a web of plans and betrayals that may wipe us all, not just battling Cain.

"Elena," I said, my voice firm. You ought not to have come here.

Why not? She questioned, her rebellious nature returning.

"Because now you're part of this," I replied. And Cain does not leave open ends.

Her voice stumbled, but she did not back off. Then we will handle him jointly.

I gave my head a shake. "Your fight is not this one."

She said, her voice steely, "It's now."

And I realized then that she was not stoppable.

Elena.

Ryker said nothing as I exited the den, but I felt his gaze fixed on me, the weight of his silent words.

Though I couldn't leave, I was in too deep now. Not when I could have predicted it.

The night seemed cooler as I entered the lane, the shadows darker. Until it was too late, I did not notice the figure prowling in the darkness.

My pulse thumping in my chest, a hand clamped over my lips pulled me back into the darkness.

Elena.

The voice had a deep, ominous quality.

Cain."

# Chapter 9
# The Rival Alpha Shows Up

Elena

Strong, relentless fingers on my lips, earthy scent of blood and soil assaulted my senses. My instincts shouted at me to resist, but as I turned in his hands I understood how useless it was.

"Quiet," the guy said, his voice low and gruff. Until you want this to become messy.

I stopped; my pulse was racing. His hold strong yet deliberates, he pulled me further into the alley's gloom. Whichever he was, he made no one single wasted motion.

"Let me go," I growled as his hand slid from my lips to my arm.

He laughed faintly in low tones. Fishy. Ryker's very focused, which makes sense.

My stomach turned over at Ryker's name.


"who are you? "I insisted on this.

His face came out of the shadows suddenly, and I first could see him properly. He had sharp features and eyes that appeared to gleam softly in the low light; he was broad-shouldered.

It took little time to put his overpowering, stifling presence together.


I mumbled, "Cain."

My skin crawled at the smile he wore over his face. "He says about me? I am flattened.

"What are your preferences? The "

Based on you? Though it didn't reach his eyes, his smile grew wider. "Not really much. from Ryker, though? Everything.

Ryker

Something was awry the once I entered the alley and smelled her.

Elena? I phoned, my voice quiet yet firm.

The quiet was deafening, and my wolf roused restlessly under my skin, its roar pulsing through my chest. My senses acute, I pushed forward into the darkness and spotted them then.

Cain was having hers.

She was pushed against the wall, her defiance clear in her eyes through her terror. Cain's smile became wider as he looked at me, then he pushed in her direction as if he was challenging me to act.

" Ryker," he said, his voice sarcastically laid back. "So great of you to come see us."

"Let her go," I murmured, sounding as low a snarl.

" Why should I? "Cain retorted. "Isn't she the reason you're slipping? The reason your pack began to question you. Ryker, her vulnerability is evident. And flaws must be gone from us.

Rage blinded my eyes, so I went forward with clinched fists. You touch her; I will tear you apart.

Cain chuckled, the sound chilly and contemptuous. "He's right there. Alpha I have been waiting for.

He let her go suddenly, grinningly pushed her toward me. I grabbed her and straightened her as she staggered into my arms.

"Don't worry," Cain responded, his voice loaded with malice. "I'll be seeing you soon."

And he vanished into the darkness, leaving only the echo of his warning.

Elena

Though my hands was trembling, I refrained from showing it. Ryker held my arms firmly, anchoring, yet it was difficult to ignore the storm in his gaze.

"Are you doing okay? His voice was gentler than I would have imagined when he asked.

I lied and said, "I'm fine."

His tone tightening, he added, "You shouldn't have been here."

I shot back, "Neither should you." But right now, we're here.

His jaw locked and I could see the conflict screaming within him. Though he saw it was too late, he sought to shield me from all of this.


"What with you does Cain wish for? I said.

"Control," he replied, his voice calm yet strong. "He wants my life, territory, pack. He will also demolish everything that's in his path.

Including me, I added, the awareness striking me like a freight train.

Ryker spoke nothing, but his silence said volumes.

Ryker

My head whirling with the ramifications of Cain's action, I hurried her out of the alley fast. Having involved Elena, he had crossed a boundary, and I couldn't get rid of the impression that this was just the start.

I stopped her at her apartment right at the entrance.

You have to remain out of this, I stated with a stern voice.

Her eyes ablaze with defiance, she turned to face me. You know that's not going to happen.


Elena

"Don't," she interrupted me off saying. "You're not allowed to decide for me.

Tucked between knowing she was right and wanting to shield her, I glanced at her.

" Fine," I answered at last. "But you must know what you're up against if you're going to be involved."

Her countenance changed to include a nod. "Tell me everything."


Caleb

From the terrace, I observed them and started to smile satisfactorily.

Ryker reasoned he could outmaneuver me and keep her safe. He was misled, however.

This transcended mere territory or authority. This was about little by bit breaking him until nothing remained.


She was the key as well.

Elena

Ryker's justification was both horrible and intriguing. Cain was a predator, merciless and relentless, not only a competitor alpha. His intention was to totally destroy Ryker, not just seize his pack.

And you're simply going to let him? I asked, my voice somewhat angry.

Ryker's jaw clenched. "I am not letting him act. But should I make a mistake, my pack suffers.

"What then is the scheme?'"

He paused, and I could sense his weight of obligation bearing down on him. "I do not yet know."

Though honest, that was not the response I was looking for.

Ryker

With a sad heart, I left her place carrying my restless wolf under my skin. Cain had moved; I knew it would not be his last.

When I got back to the den, the pack was waiting with obvious anxiety.

"What transpired? "Milo narrowed his brows and inquired.

"Cain," I muttered, the one word sufficient to set forth a chorus of whispers.

"What is he looking for?"

I looked at Milo and spoke steadily. All.

The pack became quiet; their fury and dread simmered just under the surface.

Milo responded, his voice firm, "We cannot keep waiting." "He's going to separate us if we wait too late. Act now."

I know, I remarked. We shall then act. But we do things my way.

"Your way hasn't been working," Milo lashed back.

Although the conflict between us buzzed like a live wire, I stayed firm.

"We'll deal with Cain," I replied, speaking deliberately. But we play none of his games. Not now.

Milo said nothing, but the uncertainty in his eyes was tough to overlook.

Elena.

I stayed up unable to fall asleep. I haunt Cain's words, his smile, the icy dread in his gaze.

But my waking state was not just driven by anxiety. It was the awareness that I was in too deep and that, even if I wanted to, I could not flee.

Ryker's world was seductive even if it was perilous. And, as much as I hated to admit it, the conflict drew me in more than his person.

I only prayed it wouldn't ruin me.

Targeting Ryker's pack directly, Cain's next action forces Ryker and Elena to face the mounting threat together.

# Chapter 10
## Pulled to the Mystery

Elena

Some individuals seek solutions out of obligation. Some follow them in search of justice. For me, it was something more profound—something I couldn't really name.

Ryker was a riddle, a jigsaw I could not quit assembling. My knot in his universe became more complex the more I knew. Pulling away grew tougher the closer I got.

And Cain now belonged in that world as well. His icy gaze, his mocking smile, the way he had used me to transmit a message—all stayed in my consciousness, a continual reminder of how deep I had dropped into the darkness.

But I stopped nowhere.

I would not stop either.

I was not attracted to Ryker alone. Everything he stood for, everything he was working to defend drew me in.

Even yet, it required risking myself to grasp it.

Ryker

She was going to die personally.

When I saw her squared shoulders and jaw set when she entered the Lower District the next morning, that my first thought. She belonged nowhere, not in this area of the city, not in my world.

She was there, however, defying every caution, every rationale as if she was determined to expose all my secrets.

From the darkness, I watched her as my wolf stirred with equal parts frustration and something more. Something I could afford to feel.

Stopped in front of the ancient market booths, she looked around as if she was looking for someone.

Then, as if she could feel me, her eyes fixed on mine.

We neither moved for a second. The sound of the market vanished, the globe shrinking to just the two of us.

She hardly seemed astonished to see me. She seemed, if anything, exactly as anticipated.


Elena

Rising from the darkness, he moved deliberately yet with fluidity like a predator. He attracted notice even amid the anarchy of the market.

You're following me right now? His voice was dry, but his eyes was keen.

"Not everything's about you, Ryker," I fired back, crossing my arms. "But since you're here...."

"Let me guess," he interrupted me off saying. You want answers.

I bent my head to examine him. "Maybe I want to know why you keep avoiding them."

His smile vanished, and for a second something fluttered in his face. maybe vulnerability. Alternatively regret.

"You shouldn't be here," he murmured, his voice softening now.

"Neither should you," I said.

The conflict between us buzzed like a live wire, and I could feel the pull—the unspoken bond neither of us wanted to acknowledge.

He said, "You're going to get yourself hurt."

Then tell me the truth, I said, approaching closely. "Of what are you most terrified?""

Ryker

Her comments land more forcefully than they ought.

For what was I terrified of? Her simple response was the one.

She was fire, blazing too near and too brilliantly. And I was the stupid person who kept reaching for her knowing it would ruin me.

I answered at last, "I can't."

"Why not?" asked. She insisted, her voice faintly annoyed.

"Because the truth will change everything," I replied. And you may not be ready for it.

Her brows furrowed, but before she could reply, someone yelled loudly close by.

I turned, my senses heightening as I looked around the assembly. Two males was shouting loudly enough to attract notice while debating next to one of the booths. But the aroma caused me to become tense, not the debate.

Cain's men.

"Elena," I exclaimed with a sharp urgency. You must go. presently.

"What? Why is that? '

I replied, taking her arm and dragging her toward the edge of the market, just leave.

But one of the guys turned, his eyes fixed on me before we could go too far.

" Ryker!"

Bad it.



Elena

The next few minutes passed in a haze.

Ryker moved quicker than I could have imagined the guy sprang for us. With his body coiled like a spring, he threw me behind him and squarely confronted the menace.

Ryker snipped, his voice low and nasty, "You shouldn't have come here."

The guy grinned, his posture going toward something predatory. " Ryker, you have been a pain in Cain's side for far too long. Time to take care of you.


Ryker didn't reply. He had no need of it.

The struggle broke out quickly and violently like a hurricane. Ryker moved with a fluidity and nearly superhuman accuracy, his attacks deliberate.

Still, the guy was robust and not alone.

Another stranger grabbed me from behind before I could respond.

Elaine! Ryker's voice was piercing; his focus shot to me.

I battled, my training guiding my elbow into the ribs of my assailant. He grumbled and released go; I pivoted to strike a strong kick to his knee.

Ryker muttered, finishing off the first guy, "Not bad," a trace of enjoyment in his voice.

"Thanks," I responded, panting. "What then?

"Now we run," he murmured, snatching my hand.

Ryker

Though I knew them better than anyone, the Lower District's lanes was a labyrinth. Elena followed me around the curves, my senses sharpened to find any indication of pursuit.

My chest heaving, we halted at last, buried in the darkness of an old warehouse. I looked to her.

Are you alright? "I asked."

Though her voice was wobbly, she said, "I'm fine."

I looked at her, trying to find any indication of remorse or terror. All I saw, however, was will.

"You ought to have stayed away," I replied, my voice lower now.

And miss all this as well? Trying to lighten the situation, she remarked "Neither a chance."

Still, I nearly grinned despite everything. Almost rather.

Elena

He was untouchable. Angry and overly protective, but also something more.

Looking at him, standing there with the weight of the world on his shoulders, I became aware of how far I had fallen.

Ryker, you're not alone in this; my voice is steady.

He fixed me, something unsaid between us. "I am aware."

Still, the sound of approaching feet broke off the moment.

His voice harsh, he replied, "They found us." "Stay close," says.

The battle was still in progress.

Neither was the mystery that pulled us together.

Ryker's fight with Cain's soldiers becomes more intense as he starts to show more of his was wolf side to protect Elena. Cain's intentions for Ryker's pack and Elena's father's participation start to show themselves meantime.

# Chapter 11
# The Gala Heist

Ryker

The gala was a chessboard, each piece exactly positioned. Under shimmering chandeliers, the rich mingled and their laughter reverberated throughout the great ballroom. It was an image of luxury and of control. But here control was a mirage, as delicate as the glass in their champagne glasses.

I had not come to rejoice. Here I was ready to choose.

The target tonight was a vault buried under the estate, guarded behind layers of protection meant to keep individuals like me out of reach.

Not one thing, nevertheless, was impossible. The secret to that vault would not only unlock additional doors but also buy my pack the leverage required to keep Cain away.

The schedule was straightforward. In, pick the key, and go before anybody saw.


Her wasn't anything I had considered.


Elena

I turned away from these galas. The forced grins, the false laughing, the way everyone pretended not to see my father hovering over the throng like a silent police officer. I wanted no part of it; everything was politics, a game of appearances.

Tonight, however, was not about what I desired.

As we entered the ballroom, my father cautioned us to keep our eyes alert. "Tonight, there are a lot of very significant people here, not all of them friends."

I nodded, not sure he was speaking to me specifically. Never showing more than he had to, my father always played his cards near the chest. It was among the few topics on which we disagreed most famously.

Still, I felt as if tonight something was amiss. The air seemed weighted, packed with an unidentified tension.

And then I saw him.


Ryker

The tuxedo was uncomfortable; the neck was too tight; the cloth was too stiff. Still, it fulfilled its function by mixing me into a throng I wasn't supposed there.

I kept my motions laid back and went around the room like a ghost, grudgingly smiling when needed. Every second on the clock was getting me closer to the window of opportunity I could not afford to overlook.


The air changed, and she materialized.


Elena.

She was gorgeous; her clothing, a rich emerald green, accentuated her eye fire. Her head held high, her presence dominating even in a room packed of power players. She walked deliberately.

Her gaze then turned directly on me.

The world shrank for a minute, the sound of the gala vanishing into the background. Neither did I nor did she turn aside.

I knew I ought to have vanished into the throng before she could make the connections. I did not, however.

I could not.


Elena

Looking away from him was difficult for some reason. He was not among the polished elites and smooth-talking politicians here. But he went across the room as if he owned it, each stride deliberates, each gaze measured.

And then it occurred to me.

The alley man's man. The burglar.

My heart stopped a beat and I experienced an adrenaline surge. He was doing what right here?


I said, "Excuse me," passing a gathering of visitors and headed for him.

When he spotted, me arriving, I briefly feared he may escape. Rather, he remained where he was, a smile pulling at the edge of his mouth.

"Fancy seeing you here," he remarked in a low, seductive voice.

Keeping a calm voice, I added, "Cut the act." "This's where you're working?""

"Enjoying the party," he added, his smile becoming wider.

I responded, moving closer, "Try again."

His gaze strayed to something over my shoulder, and I noticed for the first time a fracture in his façade.

"Walk with me," he replied, his voice abruptly austere.

He grabbed my arm and led me toward the room's edge before I could object.


Ryker

Though plans often fell apart the minute you started them, I hadn't intended to include her.

"Elena," I said, lowering my voice. You have to go. Not now.

"Not until you tell me what's going on," she responded, her eyes flashing with will.


Time for this was not available. The vault was waiting; the more time I spent here, the more perilous this became—for both of us.


"You belong nowhere here," I replied. also, neither do I.


She scowled, clearly annoyed. "so why are you in here?""

"Because I have to be," I answered, speaking softly now. However, you do not. Head home, Elena. Kindly.

Her teeth closed tightly, and her eyes showed struggle. She was not going away, yet she did not trust me.

A voice shriveled in my ears before I could say anything more.

" Ryker, you have limited time.

Tensing, the reminder pulled me back to reality.

Steering clear of her, I said, "Go."

She never did, however.

She instead trailed after me.

Elena

Although I had no idea what I was anticipating, this was not it.

He walked confidently through the estate's rear hallways, as if he had visited before. Every action was purposeful, every look over his shoulder crisp and calculated.

"What do you have in mind? My heart beating, I murmured.

"Trying to save my people," he added without looking at me.

Your people?

He ignored him, and I felt the irritation rising inside me.

You're a thief, I said. You choose stuff. This's about that, not anything else.\\"

Stopping abruptly, he turned to face me and said, "It's not that simple."

Then make me understand, I said, looking at him.

I thought he may for a split second. His smile stiffened, however, as the sound of feet reverberated down the corridor.

His voice hard, he ordered, "Stay here."

He disappeared before I could debate.

Ryker

The vault was just ahead; its steel door was formidable but not unbreakable. Working fast, my fingers across the keyboard moved with trained ease.

My attention was not entirely focused on the work however.

She was quite near. very engaged. And she was in danger right now.

The lock snapped open, and I entered the vault, chilly air rushing over me. The secret was hidden within a glass case—where it ought to be.

I snatched it and tucked it into my pocket as soon as I heard activity.

"Elena,"

My pulse pounding, I shot from the vault and rounded the bend.

She was there, caught by two security officers, her face a combination of defiance and terror.

"Let her go," I murmured, sounding as low a snarl.

The guards pivoted, hands near their rifles.

They had never had a chance.


Elena

Though I had seen him fight before, this was different.

Every attack exact, every motion fluent, he moved like a predator. What struck the guards? They had no idea.


His chest heaving, he turned to me when it was finished.

"Are your kowhais voice quieter now, he asked.

I nodded, but my heart was still pounding. What now?

"Now," he replied, his face gloomy, "we run."

Ryker and Elena discover as they leave the gala that Cain has been observing them the whole time, preparing the ground for an even more lethal battle.

# Chapters 12
# Suspicions and Sparks

Elena

Since we had fled the gala, my breathing had not returned to normal. The chilly air enveloping us as we dropped into the shadows of an abandoned warehouse on the outskirts of the city seemed as if the night was closing in.

I ought to have been explosive. Furious with him for bringing me into this and for endangering me. Instead, all I could sense was the electric tension pulsing between us—a tension that had been boiling since our first encounter.

Ryker walked a few steps away, his mouth tense and his eyes searching the blackness as if he anticipated an assault. Since we had left, he had not spoken a word; the stillness was intolerable.

"Are you going to share with me what just happened? Crossing my arms, I asked at last.

His eyes flashed quick and guarded to me. You ought not to have been there.

"I'm sorry; was that an apology? I fired back, my annoyance boiling to the top. Since it definitely doesn't sound like one.

"You don't understand," he replied, his voice low but with a sharp edge that quickened my pulse. "You was there, which complicated everything."

I caught myself not turning a gala into a war. "Exactly what was you hoping to pilfer?

Enough was answered by his silence.


Ryker

She was untenable. Sharp, tenacious, and much too courageous for her own benefit.

I wanted to explain why I had to be there, why the key in my pocket meant life or death for my group, and tell her the truth. She would be more at risk, however, the more knowledge she had.

"Go home, Elena," I urged, speaking more gently this time.

Her eyelids closed and I knew she was nowhere. For me, Ryker, you do not get to determine that. Not these days.

Fighting the want to tell her everything, I tightened my hands. She asked for nothing knowing what she was looking for.

"Cain is watching me," I replied instead. Should he see you with me, he will come for you as well.

Her mouth clenched, but she did not back off. "then allow him." I have no fear of him.


Her disobedience was both seductive and frustrating all at once. I moved forward, our separation becoming smaller.


"You should be," I murmured, just above a whisper.


Elena

Though I refused to let him know how much he changed me, his words shivered down my spine.

"What then are you not telling me? My voice now softer, I asked.

He turned to face me then, actually looked at me, and for a second I sensed something raw in his gaze. anything fragile.

"Everything," he said, his voice so low I almost missed it.

There was heated air between us, the weight of unsaid facts precariously poised.

The sound of an automobile engine rang over the distance before I could say anything. Ryker's head shot toward the sounds, his whole body stiffening like a predator poised for attack.

His voice harsh, he replied, "They found us."

"Who?"

He grabbed my arm and shouted, "Cain's men." "We must relocate." currently.

Ryker

With my senses sharpened, the city's passageways melted together as I guided Elena through the labyrinth. Behind us, their footfall resounding in the darkness, their smells distinct and unambiguous.

I said, "Stay close," looking over my shoulder to see she was keeping up.

She said nothing, but I could sense her will and her will to allow fear stop her.

As we turned a corner, I saw an ancient service door leading to a subterranean tunnel. Though not perfect, it was our best shot.

I pushed the door open and hauled her into here.

The air in the gloomy tube was stale. Pressing my back against the wall, I listened as the footsteps became louder before stopping.

"They're close," Elena said in a whisper.

I answered, my voice low, "I know."

We stood silently, clearly tense between one another. And then the footsteps disappeared just as quickly as they had arrived.

I murmured, "They're gone," releasing a breath I had not noticed I had been holding.

"For now," she replied, her voice consistent in all circumstances.

Elena

The tunnel's quiet was deafening; the gloom pressed in all around us. His chest heaving, I leaned against the wall and tried to catch my breath.

Breaking the quiet, I whispered, "You've done this before."

"Too many times," he said, sounding exhausted.

His voice carried something that caused my heart to hurt—a tiredness that suggested wars waged and lost.

What makes that key so crucial? I queried.

His mouth closed and I could see effort in his eyes. Though he knew I would not stop asking, he did not want to tell me.

At last he remarked, "It's leverage." Something Cain cannot afford to lose.

And you're pilfering it for your pack?

He nodded, staring right at me. "All I have is them."

His voice carried something raw, a sensitivity he was unable to conceal.

Then you're all I have, he said softly.

The words lingered there, heavy and silent.

Ryker

Why I stated what I did not know. Perhaps it was her attitude toward me—that of someone attempting to comprehend a world she did not belong in. Perhaps it was the way she made me feel—that I was not alone.

She answered nothing, but she also did not turn away.

"Elena," I replied, approaching further closely. "Your fight is not this one."

"It's now," she responded, her voice firm.

Though I couldn't deny the fire in her eyes, her resistance was frustrating. She was not going to go, and part of me wanted her not to.

I could not let her suffer however.

The sound of feet resounding down the corridor before I could say anything more.

"Time's up," I remarked, my voice harsh. "We have to get going."

She nodded with a firm look.

And together we vanished into the night.

Ryker and Elena find that Cain has created a trap for Ryker's pack as they flee his soldiers, therefore forcing Ryker to make a decision that can destroy their delicate trust.

# Chapter 13
## Ryker's' Dilemma

Ryker

Actions. They were the negative aspect of leadership. Every choice I took affected my flock and bound them to either good or negative results. That weight of that obligation felt more weight tonight than it has ever done.

Although we had fled Cain's troops, the threat was not yet gone. Elena strolled next to me; her quiet spoke more loudly than words. Though I could see the questions simmering under her cool façade, I was unable to give her the desired responses—not all of them.

Not without pulling her more into the gloom that now permeated my existence.

But the truth had a way of wriggling out, no matter how firmly I tried to keep it under control.


Elena

There was obvious conflict between us, each stride across the black streets loaded with unsaid words laden with meaning. Since we entered the tunnel, Ryker had remained silent; his face was inscrutable, his motions sharp and determined.

I understood he was a man divided. Driven between his obligation to his pack and the secrets he was so fiercely guarding.

"where are we heading? I broke the quiet at last and inquired.

"To the den," he replied without looking at me, "it's safer there."

"For someone?""

He paused then to turn to face me. Something I couldn't quite describe flared in his eyes: maybe frustration. Maybe guilt.

"Elena," he remarked in a quiet voice. "You do not have to do this."

Indeed, I do, I shot back. "After what I have witnessed, you think I will just turn away? After all I have gone through?

His mouth closed, and I could see effort in his eyes. Though something was holding him back, he wanted to drive me away.

At last he responded, "It's not that simple."

Then make it basic, I said. Tell me the straight truth, Ryker. Actually, what's going on?

Ryker

The actuality. That presented the issue, not sure exactly.

The reality was neither straightforward or tidy. It was messy and dangerous, a web of lies and betrayals caught me long before I had ever met her.

I could not, however, keep her in the dark permanently.

"There is a trap," I added, my voice subdued. "Cain sets it for me, but my pack is right in the crosshairs. He's aware that

I will do anything it takes to keep them safe, even if it means marching right into his clutches.

Her eyelids opened, and I could see the pieces fitting together.

You took the key for this reason, she said. "It's leverage".

I answered by nodding. "That's the only thing separating my pack from Cain's wrath."

She said nothing at all for a minute. She then moved nearer, her voice calm. "What then is the scheme?'

Elena

The concept. That was the portion he was still working on and the one he was not mentioning. I could see it in the stiffness in his stance and in the way his eyes flicked toward the darkness.


You do not have one, do you? I probed.

Enough was answered by his silence.

Ryker—"

Cut me off, he replied, "I'll figure it out."

I could not control the mounting irritation within me anymore. "You cannot do this by yourself," I replied. You're not obliged of course.

He turned to face me then, really looked at me, and for a little instant I thought he may allow me in.

Then his face stiffened and he looked aside.

This's my struggle, he said.

Steering in front of him, I responded, "No." "It isn't." This's
ours.


Ryker

Her comments had more impact than I would have wished
to acknowledge. She had no idea what she was saying or
what it meant to stand with me in this.

My voice softer now, I added, "You don't know what you're
asking for."

Then show me, she murmured, her eyes fixed.

I tightened my hands; the wolf inside of me restless. She was
too connected, too near, yet the idea of driving her away
seemed impossible.

" Fine," I answered at last. But you have to go with my lead.

Her lips twisted into a little, determined grin. "I think I can
handle that."


Elena

The den turned out not as intended.

It was buried under the remains of an old warehouse in the
neglected sections of the city. The air inside smelled of moist
stone and something more, something wild.

Ryker's pack was waiting for him; their looks combined relief with discomfort. They did not trust me; I could not hold them responsible.

A tall, broad-shouldered guy said sharply, "She shouldn't be here."

"Milo," Ryker remarked, his voice threatening.

"She's a liability," Milo said, discounting him. "Cain will turn around and attack us."

Ryker moved closer and remarked, "She's not a liability." She's right here with me.

Though the words shocked the crowd, it was the manner he uttered them—firm, relentless—that made my heart contract.

I was not just present here. I stood in for him.

Ryker

The group moved restlessly, clearly afraid. Milo's comments hovered in the air, a challenge I could not afford to let slip.

I continued, my voice firm, "Elena's here because she can help us." "Neither Cain nor us fight fairly. She's knowledgeable in things we can use but not in others.

Though his jaw hardened, Milo refrained from arguing. Though none of them spoke, the others cast nervous looks at one another.

For now, that was sufficient.

Where is the remainder of the pack? I asked, turning the conversation elsewhere.

"They're scattered," Milo said. "Cain's guys have been observing the regular locations. We have to continue to move.

Then we must go quickly, I said. We cannot allow Cain get the upper hand.

Elaine

I observed Ryker as the pack started to plot. Here he was different; his presence was imposing, his voice serene even in the tumult all around him.

He was not only an alpha or a burglar. He had leadership.

And he was bearing a load nobody else seems to be aware of.

I discovered him standing by himself, gazing out into the darkness beyond the den, when the group called to adjourn.

"You're not only fighting Cain," I broke the quiet. You're battling yourself.

He said nothing, but the strain in his shoulders indicated I was correct.

"Whatever you're hiding," I murmured, approaching closely. You do not have to accomplish anything by yourself.

Then he turned to me, his face insensible. Elena, you believe you can rescue me?"

I answered, "No." But I believe we can help one another.

Between us, the words hung weight fully and silently.

I also noticed something in his eyes for the first time that I had not seen before.

Expectations.

A pack betrayal drives Ryker to doubt who he can trust as he gets ready for Cain's next action, so endangering Elena more than ever.

# Chapter 14
## Elena's First Signal

Elena

I was not the kind to back off and wait for responses to flow to me. Early on, I had discovered that one had to go out and get the truth if one sought it.

And just now, Ryker's universe—a reality that seemed very vital yet made no sense—buried the truth.

Ryker's pack was strewn in their corners, the den had descended into a tense silence, and the den spoke in low voices or grimly determined sharpening of weapons. Ryker himself had vanished into the darkness, clearly tense.

That left me on my own.

Not quite by myself, though. Milo's eyes tracked me everywhere, his mistrust weighing me in impossible ignore.

You do not think I am a spy? Crossing my arms, I asked, catching him staring straight across the room.

"I think you belong nowhere," he said bluntly. You have clouded Ryker's judgment.

"Maybe you should trust him," I said, squarely facing his glare.

Milo gave a snort and turned aside. "I believe Ryker." You're not someone I trust.

I had to show him incorrectness.

I had to find something, anything, that might tip the scales in our favor if I wanted to assist Ryker—and win even a shred of his pack's trust.

I therefore got to work excavating.

The lair was a tangle of secrets, half-finished maps, and hurriedly sketched ideas. It wasn't organized, but it was thorough. Ryker's pack had been watching Cain for months, piecing together his movements and unraveling his network one thread at a time.

But one paper struck my attention.

A solitary sheet, nestled behind a heap of papers. A symbol I'd seen before—a crescent moon interwoven with a wolf's head.

The same symbol I had discovered in the warehouse.

Ryker

Before I saw her, I sensed her presence—the faint buzz of her pulse piercing the silence of the lair.

Stepping inside the room, I said, "Elena."

She turned, the paper in her palm, her gaze keen and interrogating.

"This's what is happening. She held it up and asked.

My chest became tighter. "Where in particular did you discover that?

Does it really matter? She said, "She refuted." "What does it imply?"

I was not inclined to inform her. Not because I didn't trust her, but because the truth would drive her further into the darkness I'd been trying to keep her out of.

But I could see in her eyes that she was not going to let this
go.

At last I remarked, "It's Cain's mark." "That's how he runs
his people. It's a warning more than just a symbol.

"A warning regarding what?"“

"For everyone who opposes him," I added, my voice low. He
leaves it behind to show his adversaries what lies ahead.

Elena

His words sunk in and my tummy turned around.

The symbol was a threat, not just a hint.

"Why did you not tell me this earlier? My voice harsher than
I had meant, I asked.

He added, clearly frustrated, "Because it's not your fight."

Right now, I said.

He shook his head, his jaw clenching. “You don't
understand what you're getting into, Elena. Cain doesn't
play fair. If he knows you're involved—”

“Then he'll come after me,” I concluded for him. “I'm not
afraid of him, Ryker.”

"You should be," he murmured, his voice barely above a whisper.

The intensity in his gaze stole my breath away, but I didn't back down. "We can stop him. Together."

For a minute, he didn't answer. And then, eventually, he nodded.

Ryker

You're correct, darling.

The least I could do since she already lived in danger was make sure she understood what she was up against.

Pointing to the paper in her palm, I added, "This mark indicates he's preparing something significant. He makes sole use of it just before he moves.

"What type of action?

"A hostile one," I remarked. For his adherents, it serves as a rallying cry. An assault is what it means.

Her eyes became wider. "An attack directed on who?"""

"On us," I murmured, my voice dark. "He's coming for the pack."


Elena

After his remarks, the weight of what we was facing sank down on me and the air seemed thicker.

"What then is our action? "I inquired, my voice firm even as anxiety crept in.

"We fight," Ryker remarked, without adding anything.

He stated it as if it was the only choice; the concept of surrender was not even feasible.

Perhaps it wasn't as well too.

"I want to volunteer," I replied.

"You're aiding," he said.

"No," I said, approaching further closely. "I mean truly helpful." Let me act. Let me fight for you.

His face softened, and I could see struggle in his eyes. Elena, this's not your struggle.

It's now, I insisted forcefully.

He ignored me for a time. He nodded at it too. Alright, he said. But you go with my guidance.


Ryker

Though I couldn't resist it longer, bringing her into the conflict carried some danger. We needed every edge available if Cain was here for us.

And Elena was a benefit for all her resistance.


My pack hushed as we walked into the room, I lead her to the others. Milo squinted his eyes but said nothing.

"Cain's planning an attack," I remarked, speaking deliberately. We must be ready.

The pack mumbled among themselves as the room became tense.

"And Elena?" Milo inquired, his voice cutting. "What is she doing right now?"'

"She's with me," I added, not elaborately.

There was no space for debate in the statements, and Milo refrained from pushing.

For just now.


Elena

On paper at least, the idea seemed straightforward. With the knowledge we have, follow Cain's moves, predict his next action, and stop him before he could strike.

But basic plans seldom ever remained that way.

I was more and more uncomfortable as the group got ready. Ryker was composed, deliberate, yet I could see the strain in his shoulders from his jaw tightening when he believed no one was watching.

For him, this struggle was personally relevant.

And then it became personal for me as well.

A pack treachery threatens to destroy everything as Ryker and Elena work to put Cain's plot together, therefore exposing them to Cain's approaching assault.

# Chapter 15
# The Trap Sharpens

Ryker

Trust was not a strong thing. In my universe, it was less robust than glass—easily broken and hard to put back together.

Perched on the brink of the den, I stared into the blackness of the forest beyond. The evening was quiet, too quiet, the air heavy with the type of tension before a storm.

Cain was closing in on things. It seemed obvious to me. The worst of all is also the impression that someone on the inside was guiding him persisted.

I replied without turning, knowing Elena behind me.

She continued, leaning closer, "you cannot keep doing that."

"What are you doing?"

"Shutting me out," she replied, her voice more than usual harsh. "We must fight Cain collectively if we're to accomplish it at all. That covers trusting me as well.

I turned then to meet her sight. Her eyes glowed with fire, will burning more brilliantly than mine uncertainties.

Quietly, I murmured, "It's not you I don't trust."

Her face relaxed, and for a little while the weight of everything we were dealing with seemed less weighty.

Still, the moment didn't last.

Elena

Any Ryker had been about to say was cut off by the sound of feet. Milo showed up, his face stern and his attitude incomprehensible.

His voice low, he replied, "We have a problem."

Ryker's mouth closed tightly. "What is it?"

"Scouts reported Cain's men close to the northern border," Milo remarked. "They're getting ready for camp.

A cold crawled over my back. "He's close."

"Too close," Ryker replied, his voice sharp.

Milo paused, his eye darting to mine. "And there's something else."

'What? Ryker insisted.

Milo's look became darker. "Someone has been giving him material. He's familiar with our gestures.

The words floated around like a bomb just ready to detonate.


Ryker

Worse than I had imagined was it. A mole in the pack was not just a nuisance; if we failed to eradicate them, it was death sentence.


"who? "My voice was stern as I asked.


"We still don't know," Milo remarked. Nonetheless, whomever it's, they're terrific. For weeks Cain has one step ahead of us.

Just under my skin, the wrath boiled, my wolf chewing to the surface. My pack meant to be a family. This treachery went further than I could have ever imagined.

"We'll find them," I answered, speaking steadily. They will regret it too when we do.

Milo nodded, but his uncertainty was hard to overlook.

Elena

The meeting was tense, the air heavy with mistrust and hardly containing wrath.

"Who would you guess it's? Once Milo went, I asked Ryker.

With a clipped tone, he responded, "I'm not sure." but I'll find out.

I paused, my own concerns weighing down on me. "Do you think Milo could be—?"

Ryker answered straight out, "No." "He's loyal regardless of our differences."

Although his confidence was comforting, it did not lessen the risk in the scenario.


"What if that someone you trust is involved? I questioned.


Ryker's teeth clenched, and I could see struggle in his eyes. Then they're not who I had assumed they was.


Ryker

Over the following two hours, we pored over ideas attempting to predict Cain's next action. But every plan seemed inadequate, every concept weakened by the awareness that someone was working against us from the inside.

I was not nearer solutions by the time the sun started to rise.

Turning to her, "Elena," I said. Perched at the side of the room, she was carefully reviewing one of the maps we had been working on.

She raised her weary but targeted gaze.

You should get some rest, I said.

"So, should you," she shot back.

I nearly let out a grin. Almost.

But the sound of rising voices came from the corridor before I could answer.


Elena

The quarrel pulled us both to our feet, the strain cracking like a live wire.

Ryker left before I could say anything, and I followed closely.

When we arrived to the cause of the disturbance, Milo and another pack member—Tessa—was embroiled in a furious argument.

You believe I have no idea what you have been doing? Milo hissed, his voice harsh enough to slice across the air.

Tessa shot back, her eyes burning, "you know nothing."

"Something is happening. Ryker insisted, silence falling over the room.

With a clenched jaw, Milo turned to face him. "She's the Mole."

The charge floated about like a bomb just ready to go off.

Ryker

Tessa opened her eyes, clearly shocked. "That's a falsehood! Her voice quivering, she said. I would never turn against the pack.

Milo crossed his arms with a hard-pressed attitude. Then how can Cain know our every movement? You're the one who has been slipping off at night while someone else is providing him information.

Tessa turned to look at me, begging eyes. Ryker, you know me. I would not follow through on this.

My wolf roused, the room's tension heavy and stifling. I peered between them, my instinct guiding me to see more than first greeted the eye.

"Milo," I murmured, my voice calm. "For what evidence do you have?

"She's the only one leaving the den without telling anyone," Milo added.

Tessa shook her head, speaking now. "I have been compiling goods! You know how low we have been operating.

The pack was observing; their looks combined uncertainty with mistrust.

Enough, I murmured, quieting the space. "We never accuse people without evidence."

Milo's jaw locked but he refrained from arguing.

"Everybody stays on alert until we know for sure," I added. Nobody leaves the den without permission.

Elena

The tension did not release after Ryker's orders. If anything, it simply became thicker, distrust hanging in every gaze, every whispered exchange.


You believe it to be hers? Later, when we were alone ourselves, I asked Ryker.

He shook his head, his face incomprehensible. "I'm not sure. But things do not add up.


"What do you imply?"

"I mean Milo's right—Cain has someone on the inside," he remarked. "But Tessa's not the only one whose behavior has seemed odd."

His words weight sank over me, and I understood how dangerously this situation had become.

None was safe if Cain had crept into the pack.

Not even Ryker, not even

Ryker finds a mysterious note left behind in the den as pack tensions rise that suggests a betrayal closer than he would have ever anticipated, therefore endangering Elena and the pack.


# Chapter 16
## The Bonds Deepens

Elaine

Trust was not something I found natural. It never has. But trust seemed like a decision I lacked the luxury of avoiding with Ryker.

Following the argument between Milo and Tessa, the stress in the den was intolerable. Everybody was on edge, their doubts sharpened like knives. The pack was tearing at the seams, and Ryker could feel its weight crushing down on him.

I discovered him in the training room working through a sequence of blows on a punching bag, his motions exact and crisp. The emptiness echoed the sound of his hands striking the heavy canvas.

Leaching against the doorframe, I murmured, "You're going to wear yourself out."

He stopped without even looking at me, saying, "I'll be fine."

"That's not what I meant," I murmured, approaching closely. "You're carrying too much, Ryker. You're not working alone here.

His chest heaving, he stopped then turned to face me. His eyes blazed with irritation, but also there was something raw and unprotected there.

Then, Elena, what would you advise me to do? His voice was quiet as he inquired. Trust someone who could be employed by Cain? Could my pack be in danger? '

Meeting his look, I answered, "You can trust me."

Ryker

Her remarks ground me in a manner I never would have expected by cutting through the anarchy in my head.

Elena once more She was fire—relentless, ferocious, and far too hazardous for my well-built barriers. She was, however, also the only one who appeared to see through the weight I bore and the only one not hesitant to be by my side.

Finally, my voice weaker than I wanted, I answered, "I know I can."

She came forward, the air between us electric. " Then let me assist you."

I stopped, the wolf inside of me restless. Letting her in meant placing her in even greater risk, but the idea of keeping her at arm's distance seemed unworkable.

"This's not only about Cain," I remarked, my voice low. "It has to do with my identity. My nature is what I am.

And from what standpoint are you? Her eyes steady as she asked.

I murmured, "A monster," bitter on my mouth.

She shook her head, her eye not flickering. Ryker, you're not a monster. You're a leader. a protector.

Her words strike harder than any fist could, and I let myself believe them momentarily.


Elena

The weight of everything unsaid drew us closer, and the distance between us seemed very tiny.

"You're not alone," I murmured, voice subdued but forceful. "I am with you whatever happens."

His eyes looked at me and I could sense the turmoil in his face. Though I knew he held profound traumas, he wanted to trust me.

The door creaked open before he could reply, and Milo showed up with a gloomy look.

His voice slicing through the suspense, " Ryker," he said. "We located something."


Ryker

Milo led us to the den's main area, where the rest of the pack was gathering. On the table was a piece of paper, dirt-stained, ripped and smeared edges.

I grabbed it, my chest constricting as I read the words written across it:

He's observing. The trap is set.

Though I could not identify it, the handwriting seemed recognizable.

"What in this's this? "Peering over my shoulder, Elena questioned.

"It came out of the storage room," Milo claimed. Tessa thought she discovered it.

T Jessie. As everyone looked to her, the suspense in the room got more weight.

Her voice quivering, she added fast, "I didn't write it." "I pledge, Ryker. I would not follow through on this.

I turned to her, looking for any indication of dishonesty. All I saw, however, was terror.

Elena

The room seemed as if it would blow up from the mistrust and anxiety boiling just under the surface.

Stepping forward, I remarked, "Let's think this through." Should Tessa discover the message, it would not make sense for her to discard it there. Why would she risk revealing herself?

Milo wrinkled, but I could sense uncertainty in his eyes.

Ryker responded, his voice steady: "She has a point." Tessa would not have brought the message to us if she was the mole.

Therefore, who did?" Milo inquired, his irritation obvious.

Ryker remarked, "That's what we have to work out."

Ryker

Reluctantly, the flock scattered, their discomfort hanging like a thunder cloud. Though I couldn't let it show, I could feel their uncertainty weight down on me.

Elena anchored me as we made our way back to the map room. She remained by my side.

You suppose Cain left that note? She queried.

"Perhaps," I responded. Maybe someone was attempting to warn us.

She scowled, her eyes reflecting contemplation. "someone on the inside?",,

Again, "maybe," I murmured, even though the idea chilled my spine.

If a pack member was attempting to assist us, it indicated the mole was not operating alone.


Elena.

Although the parts were beginning to fit together, the image they created was hardly evident.


"What then?" I turned to Ryker and asked.


With palms braced on the table, he peered over the chart. "We get ready". Should the trap be sprung, we must be ready for anything Cain throws at us.


"And the mole?""


"We address them when the time comes," he added, his voice strained.

The weight of the choice was clearly seen in his eyes, the toll it was taking on him. But I also saw another: resolve.

He intended not to let Cain prevail.

Ryker

As we labored, the hours extended into the evening; every strategy seemed inadequate, every movement dangerous. But there was no option for us.

Elena remained with me through it all, her presence a steadying agent.

You should relax, I said, looking at her.

"So, should you," she said, a little grin pulling at her mouth.

I nearly started to grin back. Quite nearly.

But the sound of footsteps rang down the hall before I could answer.

Milo materialized, his eyes wide and his face pallid.

"They're here," he said.

The trap had been set off.

While the identity of the mole threatens to split the pack apart from within, Cain's soldiers sweep the den and force Ryker and Elena to battle for their lives.

# Chapter 17
# Danger to Cain

Ryker

The air in the room was packed with the type of anxiety before anarchy. "They're here," Milo said, hanging in the quiet like a knife.

I was not slow. On my feet, my senses heightening as I reached for the nearest weapon—a dagger carved with run-throughs buzzed gently beneath my touch.

"Everyone, to your respective positions!" I yelled, my voice weighted with my directive.

The pack dispersed, their motions deliberate and swift. The drill was known to them. Though none of us was ready to face it, we had practiced for this very moment.

Still, Elena was the one I concentrated on.

Her eyes wide yet focused, she stood on the edge of the room.

"Elena," I replied, walking to her. You must keep out of sight.

Her voice calm, she said, "No." Not concealing is what I am doing.

"This isn't your fight—that's not your calling."

She said, "It's now," her eyes fixed on mine.

Though I wanted to plead to keep her safe, time ran out.

"Fine," I responded and handed her a knife. Keep close to me.


Elena

Everyone braced for the storm about to strike, the den turned into a swarm of motion. With the weight of the knife Ryker had handed me foreign in my palm, my pulse flew.

I lacked the fighting spirit. not like him. I was not, however, intending to be there to observe either.

The first wave of Cain's men erupted into the chamber as the sound of breaking resonated down the passageways.

Their eyes keen, their motions fluent, they moved like predators. Still, Ryker was faster.

Head-on, he confronted the first assailant with motions that blur power and accuracy. The room descended into anarchy as weapons clashed and growls filled the space.

Following Ryker closely, I tried to keep out of his path as he watched his rear.

Still, one of Cain's guys saw me.

Ryker

My wolf sprang to the surface the instant I saw the guy headed toward Elena.

He moved quickly; I moved quicker. I grabbed him and threw enough force against the wall to cause the stone to break.

"You chose the incorrect fight," I said, low and deadly.

As the guy realized his error, his eyes became wide; it was too late. With one blow, I brought him down and denied him the opportunity to heal.

Elena was holding her ground with her knife solid in her palm when I turned back to her.

"You good? "I inquired," said.

She nodded, her breaths rapid spurts. "Yeah." I'm OK.

For now, only.

Elena

The combat continued around us, the den becoming like a battleground.

Ryker moved with a natural power, his speed and strength unparalleled. But I could see the toll it was wearing on him—the tension in his motions as he repelled wave after wave of attacks.

We had to cut off this.

Milo was sitting across the room, carrying his own against two of Cain's guys.

"Milo! "I phoned and headed for him.

He turned, his eyes narrowing to meet mine. "What are you doing?!The "

" Trying to be of assistance. I cried back.

But before I could get to him, another man crossed my way.

Cain here.

Ryker

The world appeared to slow down the moment I first saw him.

Cain stood at the den's door, his presence demanding, his smile aggravating. He didn't attack or move. He just observed, his eyes darting over the anarchy like it was a performance put on for entertainment.

" Ryker," he murmured, his voice carrying over the noise.

I battled on, my attention focused only on him.

"Cain," I said, snarling.

He raised his head and started to smile broadly. "Very messy you have created here."

"This ends now," I replied, speaking steadily.

Does it? He arched an eyebrow and inquired. "Based on where I am standing, it seems as though it's just starting."

He snapped his fingers before I could reply, and the surviving assailants withdrew from the lair eerily quiet.

"Cain, what do you want for? I insisted.

He got closer, his smile changing into something worse. You know, Ryker, what I desire. Turn over the pack; I may let them live.

" Not a chance," I said.

His gaze went to Elena suddenly, and my chest contracted.

"Ah, and this must be the famous Elena," he continued, his tone full of contempt. " Daughter of the police chief. Surely the reward is rather valuable.

"Don't," I said, sounding low and threatening.

Cain laughed, but it lacked any kind of comedy. Ryker, you have made your decision. I want you prepared to cope with the fallout.

Then he vanished, into the darkness as quickly as he had first emerged.

Elena

The stillness that followed was deafening; Cain's remarks laid over the room like a veil.

I looked to Ryker, his hands clinched at his sides and his face inscrutable.

" Ryker," I replied, approaching. "What does he simply by consequences?

He said no, staring at the location Cain had stood.

" Ryker," I repeated once again, speaking softly now.

At last he turned to face me, fear and wrath blending in his eyes. He's not done. This was just a cautionary statement.

A cold crawled over my back. "What is our current situation?"""

He corrected himself, his jaw clenching. "We get ready. He will not depart without a battle the next time he visits.

Ryker and the pack are bracing for Cain's next action when a startling den treachery threatens to destroy their defenses, therefore leaving Ryker and Elena more exposed than ever.

# Chapter 18
## Dangerous Rescue

Elena

The stress in the den was stifling. Cain's invasion had left everyone on edge, their mistrust of one another poised to explode.

I lingered beside Ryker, observing him across the room as he spoke softly among Milo and a few others. Cain's warnings lingered over us like a black cloud; the pack was disintegrating and their faith was threadbare.

Then the word started to spread.

Bloodied and barely aware, one of our scouts staggered back into the den and dropped against the stone floor.

"They took her," he muttered weakly.

Ryker bent next to him, his gaze piercing and uncompromising. Someone? They grabbed who?

The scout answered, "Tessa." "Ambushed us, Cain's men." They... They stated that's your message.

My stomach collapsed. Tisa. The one person under continual suspicion—and now she was gone.

Ryker

Cain obviously wanted me to come for her. He wanted me to act, to play in his hands.

Still, doing nothing was not an alternative.

We're getting her back, I murmured, my voice calm.

Milo wrinkled, crossing his arms. You find that to be wise? This could turn out to be a trap.

Standing, I responded, "It's a trap." We cannot, however, leave her there.

"She could be the mole," Milo replied, his voice harsh.

"She's one of us," I said, my wolf whirling under my skin. We do not forsake our own unless we know differently.

Milo paused then nodded, his face gloomy.

Turning to Elena, who was observing me with a mixture of worry and resolve, you don't have to come, I said.

Her gaze became tight. You know I'm not dragging behind.

I nearly let out a grin. Nearly.


Elena

Though the idea was pulled together quickly, perfection was not possible. Unknown numbers, Cain's men was keeping Tessa at an abandoned plant on the outskirts of the city.


Ryker led the way as we proceeded under the cover of darkness, his motions exact and methodical.


With a quiet voice, he said, "Stay near me."


Whispering back, holding the knife he had handed me, "I know the drill."

Ahead the factory loomed, its corroded walls and damaged windows evidence of years of neglect. Every shadow appeared to bear a menace; the air smelled of oil and rot.

Ryker motioned for us to halt, his eyes looking about. "Two guards at the door," he added. "We gently remove them."

Milo responded, "Got it," and sank into the darkness.

Heart thumping, I kept behind Ryker as Milo sent one of the guards a quick, quiet attack.

The second guard turned, his eyes widening as Ryker materialized behind him and executed one, seamless action to bring him down.

The road was open, but my nerves was jangled.

You okay?" Ryker asked, his voice subdued."

I nodded, bringing the knife closer. "Let's accomplish this."

Ryker

Every nook of the facility, a tangle of decaying walls and rusting equipment, might be a hiding place. My senses was on great alert; the tiniest smells and noises led me across the night.

Elena remained near, her will unflinching in face of risk. She was courageous—braver than I would have expected—and that just strengthened my will to protect her.

Tessa was discovered in a tiny room close to the rear of the facility, bound to a chair, her face battered but resolute.

" Ryker," she whispered, her voice mixed with shame and relief.

"We're getting you out of here," I remarked, then went to untie her.

But before I could, the sound of footsteps resonated behind us.

"That's a trap! Tessa cried out.

The door exploded open, and Cain's soldiers swept the space.


Elena

The struggle was disorganized, a whirl of sound and movements. Ryker was a natural force, demolishing assailants with merciless accuracy, his motions the ideal mix of power and accuracy.

But there was much too many.

As best I could, I fought back; the knife in my palm seemed both alien and necessary. One of the assailants was taken down by me; another seized me with an iron-like grasp.


"Elena! Ryker spoke sharply and with terror.


He was there, dragging the guy off me and throwing him against the wall with a snarl that shivered my spine before I could respond.

"Are you ok? He questioned, his eyes darting over me for cuts.

My voice trembling, I responded, "I'm fine."

He nodded, then turned back to face the battle, but the anxiety in his eyes persisted.

Ryker

Though we were outnumbered, I was not giving up.

Every step seemed like a struggle for survival as we battled our way back across the factory with Tessa free and Milo shielding our escape.

Elena remained near; her will inspired me. She was strong—stronger than I would have given her credit for—and as I watched her stand her ground, I felt a flash of pride.

Then I came upon him, however.

Cain

At the far end of the corridor, he stood with a sneer that infuriated me and eyes glistened with hate.

"Leaving rather soon? "He phoned with a sarcastic tone.

I snipped forward, then Elena grabbed my arm.

Her voice stern, she answered, "Not now."

She's correct. We couldn't afford to remain, even if all I wanted to do here and now was to finish.

"Next time," I said, my voice low.

Cain's grin grew wider, yet he moved not to stop us.

That was almost worse.

Elena

We left the facility, our bodies beaten yet alive, our breathing laboring.

Tessa depended mostly on Milo; her injuries slowed her significantly, but her spirit remained intact.

She murmured, "Thank you," her voice subdued. "I believed... I felt as if I was done for.

Ryker nodded with an incomprehensible look. Now, you're secure.

Still, I couldn't get rid of the sense that this was far from done as we negotiated the shadows.


Cain had let us walk off.

And it indicated he was organizing something far worse.

Ryker discovers a mysterious note left behind back at the den, a direct challenge from Cain that compels him to face not just his foe but also the increasing risk to Elena and his pack.

# Chapter 19
## Investigating Motives

Elena

Back in the den, there was a lot of unsaid questions. Cain's smile as we fled stayed in my head like a warning; the rescue had been too simple.

Ryker had not said much since we got back; his stress permeated the room as he moved in front of the map table. Tessa and Milo was close; their hushes were subdued but weighed heavily with doubt.

The quiet was intolerable to me now.

"What does his endgame look like? Crossing my arms, I leaned against the wall and asked.

Ryker stopped and turned to look at me. "Control. My group is under his grasp. He wants.

"That's not all," I murmured, getting closer. Although Cain could have stopped us back then, he did not. Why? "

Ryker closed his jaw clearly frustrated. "Because he's engaged in a lengthy game. He wants me sufficiently desperate to make errors.

"Then let's work out his next move before he makes it," I suggested.

Ryker

Elena made a valid point, but deciphering Cain's motivations proved more difficult than just guessing his next strike. Cain lived on manipulation, transforming people's doubts and worries into weapons; he did not operate just with raw force.

Glancing at the map laid on the table, I saw a network of black markings and red lines following Cain's movements. It resembled attempting to grab smoke.

Milo moved ahead, his words slicing over my ideas. "We cannot simply sit here and wait for him to act."

"I know," I responded, sounding more sharply than I meant.

Then, what then should we do? "Milo pushed."

I paused, the weight of the pack's trust pushing down on me. "We work out what he wants. Really, what is he looking for?

Elena

From the corner of the room, Tessa spoke softly but deliberately. "Is it not just the pack he's looking for?"

Everyone looked to her as her comments sank in weight.

"What do you imply? "I inquired," said.

She paused, looking at Ryker quickly. "Cain is not just seeking control. He wants to wipe out all that matters to you, Ryker. Your pack, your reputation; even her.

Her words lingered in the air and my chest became constricted.

Ryker remarked, his voice dark, "She's right." "Cain is not merely after authority. He craves retribution.

"For what purpose? "I enquired," said

Ryker's jaw tensed, and I could see shame flickering in his eyes.

"For what I grabbed from him," he said.

Ryker

No matter how deeply you tried to bury the past, it seemed to find you.

Cain and I had been friend's years ago, our packs together against a shared foe. Still, relationships established in desperation usually did not persist.

Cain had gone beyond a boundary that I cannot overlook. I had taken everything from him in exchange, and he had threatened my pack, violated our confidence.

His range. his adherents. His ego.

My voice low, I replied, "I made him weak." Now he's doing all he can to pay back the favor.

Elena's eyes softened but she showed only comprehension rather than sympathy.

"This's not only about you," she added. "It relates to everyone depending on you. We cannot let him succeed so.

Elena

The pieces began to fit as Ryker detailed his background with Cain. This was a struggle for more than simply land or influence. It became personal.

But there was another, illogical thing that kept bothering me.

"Why nowadays? "I inquired. "Why wait this long to pursue after you?"

Ryker wrinkled his brow, his expression deliberates. "Because he has been bolstering his army. Still waiting for the ideal opportunity.

"Or," I said, approaching the map, "because he found something—or someone—who gave him the upper hand."

As my words sank in, the room went still.

"You think the mole is providing him more than just knowledge," Ryker said.

One nodded. "If Cain's playing the long game, then whoever's helping him is a lot more involved than we realized."


Ryker

Elena's thesis simply served to aggravate me as it made too much logic.


Should Cain have someone on the inside, they was a collaborator rather than just a spy. Someone who understood the shortcomings of my pack more than anybody else.

"Start talking," I urged, staring broadly around the room. "If anyone knows anything, now's the time."

No one spoke, but I saw the flicker of unease in their eyes.

"Fine," I responded, my voice harsh. "Then we do this the hard way. Milo, double the patrols. No one leaves the den without my permission."


"And what about Cain?" Milo asked.

"We find him," I murmured, my jaw stiffening. "And we end this."


Elena

Though the pack dispersed to follow Ryker's instructions, the tension persisted.

I stayed behind, watching as Ryker stared at the map like he could will it to give him the answers he needed.

Stepping forward, I said, "You're not alone in this."

He looked at me, his manner softening. Know.

But I could see the weight he carried—doubt chewing at him.

"Ryker," I said, my voice soft. We will stop Cain whatever his plans are. Together."

His eyes met mine, and for a minute, the world seemed a bit less heavy.

"Thanks," he remarked softly.

Ryker

The quiet moment didn't last.

Milo came running into the room, his face austere. "We've got a lead."

I straightened, the strain in my chest intensifying. "Where?"

"One of the scouts spotted Cain near the southern border," Milo added. He's not by himself.

My jaw clinched.  It was too soon.  We weren't ready.

We had to seize it, however, if this was our opportunity to catch him off guard.

I advised everyone to get ready. We move now.

Milo nodded and melted down the hall.

Turning to Elena, her will reflected in her eyes.

"Stay close," I said.

Her nod was deliberate. " ALWAYS."

As Ryker and Elena lead the group to apprehend Cain, they unearth a heartbreaking fact about the mole's identity, leaving them wondering everything—and everyone—they thought they knew.

# Chapter 20
## The First Betrayal

Ryker

The woodland was peaceful, the type of silence that put my wolf on edge. The southern border loomed just ahead, the tension in the air thick enough to choke on.

Milo and a squad of scouts surrounded me, their motions subtle but accurate. Elena remained near, her fingers firmly clutching her knife. She belonged nowhere, not in the thick of this, yet I couldn't get myself to send her back.

As much as I hated to acknowledge it, this was her struggle now too.

"Cain's close," Milo said, his voice quiet. "The scout claimed he was getting ready close to the clearing."

I nodded to tell the group go proceed. Surround Cain, cut off his escape, and bring him down before he could launch whatever trap he had intended.

Plans, however, seldom made it through the first step.

Elena

Every stride across the trees seemed heavier than the previous. The air was wet, the aroma of moss and dirt blending with something sharper, something deeper.

Ryker was tight, his actions methodical, his concentration steadfast.  I kept near, my heart thumping in my chest as we got to the clearing.

We then spotted him.

Cain stood in the midst of the clearing, his arms crossed, his expression infuriatingly cocky.  His soldiers around him moved like shadows, their quiet menace.

"Ryker," Cain said, his voice cutting across the calm. "You sent the cavalry." I am flattened.

"Enough games, Cain," Ryker replied, his voice firm and quiet. "This ends now.".

Cain's smile grew wider as he slanted his head, his eyes shining with something deadly. Indeed, Ryker. You're rather predictable. Playing the hero always.

Ryker

On my back of the neck, the hairs stood on end. Cain was too poised and quiet. He came to gloat, not to fight.

"Cain, what do you want for? Keeping a cool head, I asked.

He laughed, the sound low and sarcastic. "What I have always yearned for". Your group. Your dominion. Your life.

"You will not get none of those," I advised.

Will not I? Cain's eyes slid behind me to something—or someone.

Turning, my wolf howling in my breast, I saw Milo moving forward with a grim countenance and stiff body language.

"Your activities? "I insisted.

Milo gave no response. Rather, he halted a few yards away, staring directly at me.

Ryker apologized, his voice weighed with remorse.

Then he turned to assist Cain.

Elena

The treachery struck like a gut-reversing blow. Milo: The mole was the one Ryker most trusted; he had been at his side through all.

"No," I said, gripping the knife in my palm more tightly.

Ryker tightened his whole body and curled his hands into fists at his sides. "Milo," he murmured, his voice low and lethal. "What the devil are you chasing?

Milo's eyes strayed momentarily, then he straightened, his face hardening. "I had nothing to choose from."

Ryker snipped: "There's always a choice."

Cain laughed—the sound harsh and frigid. " Ryker, you genuinely do not see it. Milo wanted to not betray you. He deceived you because you gave him no other option."

Ryker shot "Shut up, Cain," his rage hardly restrained.

Still, Cain's smile only became more pronounced.

Ryker

It seemed unbelievable. My second-in-command, most reliable friend, Milo had turned on me.

"You don't have to do this," I said, a low but steady voice.

Milo shook his head, his eyes flickering with something I couldn't exactly identify: perhaps guilt, maybe resignation. "This's already done, Ryker."

Cain gave him a shoulder clap, his smile annoying. "Smart move, really." Milo noted the writing on the wall. He understands that this fight is lost-for-you.

My wolf snarled, almost overpowering need to lash out overwhelming. But not now, I couldn't afford to lose control.

"This isn't over," I responded, staring directly at Cain.

With a sarcastic tone, he responded, "Oh, I think it's." Still, Ryker, you need not panic. When this's all over, I will properly look after what remains of your pack.

Elena

The atmosphere in the meadow was excruciating, the betrayal hanging in the air like a tangible weight.

146

Ryker didn't flinch, didn't back away, but I could see the tension in his eyes, the weight of everything slamming down on him.

And then Cain made his move.

His men sprang forward with a quick and exact flick of his hand. Ryker faced them squarely, his speed and power unparalleled, but the chances was against us.

Fighting back, my training kicked in as I struck one of Cain's guys precisely. Still, it wasn't enough.

Milo was still standing alongside Cain, watching as the pandemonium erupted, his look inscrutable.


I turned to him, my voice fierce. You would quit if you really loved this set.

He ignored me, but for a brief instant I thought I saw something flutter in his eyes.


Ryker

The struggle was vicious; every blow reminded one of what was at risk.

Though they were unrelenting, so was we. Cain's soldiers were Elena stayed still, her motions exact and quick, her will unbroken.

But the betrayal persisted no matter how hard we battled.

Milo

I cannot make sense of it. The pack was supposed to be a family, a bond stronger than blood.  And he'd ruined that trust with a single decision.

As the conflict went on, I caught sight of Cain retreating into the shadows, his sneer mocking me one final time before he vanished.

This wasn't over.  Not quite likely.


Elena

The clearing became quiet as Cain's final men withdrew, leaving a jumble of damaged trust and unresolved issues.

Ryker stood in the middle of it all, his chest heaving and his face expression invisible.

I moved forward to lay a hand on his arm. "Are you fine?"

He didn't reply immediately; his eyes stayed on the location Cain had stood.


"No," he said at last, his voice calm but firm. I will be, though.


I nodded and squeezed his arm lightly. "We will make it through here. together.

He turned to face me then, his eyes flickering with a mixture of rage, will, and something I couldn't quite identify.

148

But Milo's voice sliced through the quiet before he could reply.

He said, going forward, "I'm sorry."

The stress in the clearing broke like a wire pulled too tightly.

And everything changed in that same manner.

Milo tells Ryker the stunning truth behind his treachery—that which makes him doubt what he knew about Cain's intentions as well as the real threat they run into.

# Upcoming Series

Vol 1 – **The Beginning (Current Volume)**

Vol 2 – **Rising Tensions**

Vol 3 – **The Turning Point**

Vol 4 – **The Climax**

Vol 5 – **The Resolution**

www.ingramcontent.com/pod-product-compliance
Lightning Source LLC
Chambersburg PA
CBHW061537120726
48001CB00004B/1592